The Numbers Behind

Success in Soccer

Chest Dugger

CONTENTS

ABOUT THE AUTHOR

Chest Dugger is a soccer fan, former professional and coach, looking to share his knowledge. Enjoy this book and several others that he has written.

Free Gift Included

As part of our dedication to help you succeed in your career, we have sent you a free soccer drills worksheet. This is the "Soccer Training Work Sheet" drill sheet. This is a list of drills that you can use to improve your game; as well as a methodology to track your performance on these drills on a day-to-day basis. We want to get you to the next level.

Click on the link below to get your free drills worksheet.

https://soccertrainingabiprod.gr8.com/

DISCLAIMER

INTRODUCTION

'Football is a simple game. Twenty-two men chase a ball for 90 minutes and at the end, the Germans always win.' – Gary Lineker

Is soccer the most chaotic sport in the world? Is the interplay, the transition of possession, the speed of movement too great to be broken down into constituent elements? The use of analytics in sport is now well embedded. 'Marginal gains', the bedrock upon which the cycling coach Dave Brailsford built his greatest successes are cornerstones of most sports nowadays. But, until recently, that did not apply to the biggest sport in the world. Not in soccer. It was as though this simplest of sports is too complicated for statistics. Or that only one statistic counts, the number of times the ball hits the back of the net. 'The only statistic that counts,' there's an often used and annoying stock term. It's probably, though, not the worst in this traditional old game.

What's the most annoying phrase in soccer? There are plenty of contenders in this cliché-ridden world. One where the artistic brilliance on the pitch is rarely matched by the prosaic utterings off of it. There are exceptions, of course. In 2018, English speaking audiences often saw their enjoyment of the biggest soccer tournament on the planet, second only to the Olympics in terms of all sporting events, enhanced by the master of the tangential phrase, the commentator Clive

Tyldesley. Tyldesley has achieved almost cult status among aficionados with his odd links and bizarre facts.

Hearing him discuss the oil industry as hosts Russia stepped out to play lowly ranked Saudi Arabia in the opening game of the 2018 world cup was a veritable joy. As was his solo discussion as he debated at great length (with himself) the challenges that would face the originally named Neymar Jr if he sought to provide his father, Neymar Sr, with an appropriate father's day present. (The Brazil v Switzerland match becoming an annoying irrelevance as the complex debate developed).

But these are rarities, gems that shine even brighter for their sparseness, in the general world of football debate. On the one side we have the aforementioned banality of commentators balanced by the tunnel visioned debates from fans. (Take a look on Twitter to see quite how myopic conversations become). But leading the field in the league of the lamentable line is, of course, the pundit. Audiences outside of the UK might not be too familiar with the comedy heaven that is 'The Fast Show', but get on to google (other search engines are, of course, available), type in the search bar 'The Fast Show Ron Manager' and sit back in delight as the comedian Paul Whitehouse takes the inane, meaningless rumblings of the average pundit to new, hysterical, heights.

Which leads us back neatly to the most annoying phrase in soccer. 'He's a top, top player' is up there, and if we asked the former pro whether he was developing a stutter, or meant that the soccer genius in question was at the head of the subset of soccer stars we might call 'top' he would no doubt look askance, his jaw drop, and in a panic unleash a tirade of other pointless phrases. 'A game of two halves', 'textbook finish', 'lacking bottle', 'it only takes a second to score,' (which is not only a cliché, but an incredibly inaccurate one, since the time it takes the ball to cross the line and enter 'the onion bag' is just a fraction of a single second. While, at not quite the same time, any build up leading to the goal is a much more intricate process. As, we hope, this book will demonstrate.)

But top of this inimitable collection of the inane, so to speak, surely must be the incredibly annoying and fantastically inaccurate 'it evens itself out over the season.' Whatever 'it' might be, it definitely does not. Those fine Barcelona teams of the late noughties committed nth illegal nudges in every game. They won possession by fouling an opponent. But (because it was only a small foul, and they are, after all, Barcelona) were rarely penalized for it. That cheating – it is nothing else, although many pundits like to employ the euphemism 'professionalism' – did not come back to bite them, and the post-match analysis would never claim it would. Soccer matters even themselves out, it seems, does not apply to the best.

And so, it goes on. A player being sent off by an overzealous referee generally means loss of the game, especially if it happens before half time. That does not mean in the return fixture the disadvantaged side will have the problem evened up by the particular official running that game. The 'offside goal' or the legitimate one disallowed by VAR will not be equalized over the season.

Take Bournemouth AFC, for example. This tiny club based on the south coast of England was close to extinction a few seasons ago. Then they appointed a clever young manager, Eddie Howe, to lead them forward. He did, incredibly, and Bournemouth won promotion after promotion until they enjoyed season after season in the top flight of English football. While the likes of Manchester United were able to count on the income generated by 75000 fans filling Old Trafford, Bournemouth's tiny Vitality Stadium could accommodate a mere 12000. But still the team survived, often starting out on fire and in the top third of the league until injuries took their toll on Bournemouth's tiny squad, season on season, and the team would drift to mid table, still an astonishing achievement for a club so small. Then, in the Covid 19 chaos of the 2019 2020 season, the English Premier League introduced VAR. Or, at least, their own strangely subjective version of it.

Bournemouth ended up being relegated by just a single point, despite an amazing effort to win their last game away to Everton, 3-1. It marked the end of a genuine fairytale (another term which could easily win our 'most annoying phrase' competition.) It also marked the end of Eddie Howe's reign. He resigned just after the season ended.

But VAR is very unpopular in England. Too often decisions appear to favor bigger teams, or give decisions diametrically opposing other ones happening on the same day in different grounds. Plenty of people decided to look in more detail at how the decisions impacted on games. It turned out that Bournemouth had dropped thirteen points as a result of VAR decisions which appeared wrong, or at least inconsistent. Those additional thirteen points (along with the ones dropped by their opponents as a result of changes to the score line) would have seen Bournemouth ending up, as usual, in mid table. Certainly, rarely had they played badly during the season, and it had seemed, as commentators and pundits claimed with ever increasing desperation, to be just a matter of time before 'they got the results their play deserved', or 'things evened themselves out.' Of course, they never did. In all likelihood, Bournemouth became the first team in England, and possibly the world, to be relegated by Video Assistant Referee, rather than results over a long (especially long in the case of 2019 2020) season.

Because nowadays we don't just have to rely on 'gut feeling', like the midfield maestro who plays the perfect pass. No, we know how that pass came about, because we can analyze our creative master's playing style, his first touch, the number of times he practices making the pass, the success rate of the pass and just about everything else about his play. Just like we can examine exactly the role of VAR in Bournemouth's demise.

Soccer has bought into analytics. Reluctantly, slowly and against the sort of reactionary response that might be expected from some ex pros, soccer is being revolutionized. They may still feel a plate of fish and chips or burger and fries, alongside half a dozen bottles of beer, is the best way to recover after a match, but data is proving them wrong.

Data analysts are now a major part of every top professional club. They interact with players, advise coaches, examine the strengths and weaknesses of teams, establish likely tactical organization of different sides; even focus on what a referee might allow and penalize. Of course, the average amateur club or youth team has neither the man or woman power, nor certainly the access to highly advanced and highly expensive apparatus used in the professional game. But coaches at this level can look at the luxury homes in which their professional counterparts abide and learn lessons. The best will adapt what is happening the professional game and create their own versions to further their own team's development.

The fact is, despite the cynicism of an increasingly small but stubborn group of recidivists, old time players and managers who long for the past, whose broken noses twitch and pot bellies tighten at talk of analytics, data is here to stay. It infiltrates every aspect of the professional game, and it is improving performance, helping players stay at the top for longer, and moving the game of soccer into the modern age.

Analytics are here to stay. And this book will teach us all about this new and emerging field. We will focus on the use of statistics in the professional game, from which coaches can draw inspiration for their own use of analytics with their amateur clubs or youth teams. We will consider the evolution of analytics in the game, and discover that ground breakers have, in fact, been working with statistics, analysing them for their team's benefit, for far longer than might be imagined.

We will consider the difference good analytics can contribute to a team's success. After all, there must be something that stops the world's largest country (in terms of population) from winning the World Cup every time it is held, or the richest team in a particular league winning the championship every season.

We will offer some real case studies to illustrate our findings and look at which metrics are the most important in analyzing performance. This is something which could be of huge use to an amateur coach on a small budget and without a team of scientists to examine every aspect of a game.

As we have mentioned, analytics are more traditionally associated with other sports. We will look at why this might be and consider how soccer might address disadvantages it has in gathering metrics. We will look at the use of analytics to help individual players develop their game, and also how they can be used in determining set pieces. Take zonal marking, for example. Surely the most derided tactic since Sir Alf Ramsey did away with wide men and created his 4-3-3 structure, the wingless wonders? Yet, statistically, zonal marking is a more efficient way of defending a corner or wide free kick than the much adored 'man marking' (although a combination of approaches is better still.) Yet professional teams persist with zonal marking when the pundits criticize them for doing so. The reason? Coaches trust the data; pundits hark back to what they did in their day.

We will consider the way technology helps the collection of data and consider how we amateur coaches can design their own machines for gathering this information. We will look at how analytics can help coaches to spot new trends in soccer. How the future of the game might be determined by technology and scientists, rather than just ex-players. We will consider the fascinating subject of how the traditionalists of the game oppose the developments analytics can offer.

Which makes a good point to end our introduction and move on to the book proper. The English Premier league is widely considered as the biggest league in the world. It is certainly the richest. Thirty-five year ago English soccer was in the doldrums. Appalling pitches – farm fields from November to March – stultified the development of technique from grass roots level (there's an ironic turn of phrase; how coaches would have loved any sort of grass to train and play on) to professional standard. The breakdown of civil society was epitomized on the soccer terraces, hooliganism making English football a dirty term across the globe, and finally getting English teams banned from Europe. Prime Minister Margaret Thatcher hated football, and all it represented. She had already encouraged schools to sell off their playing fields to property developers, and would have loved nothing more than to ban the game altogether.

The beautiful game had turned sour. Soccer seemed destined for destruction. Within fifteen years, it was the envy of the world. The man who brought about this transformation more than any other is almost definitely the visionary Arsenal coach, Arsene Wenger, who now holds a developmental role with FIFA.

It was Wenger who brought science into his coaching; diet, stretching, training based on data. He had started the process during his days as the successful coach of an almost unknown side in the French league, Monaco, whom he led to huge success. Players who played under him speak of his genius, and the gratitude they feel for the way he extended their careers is clear even today. Those who did not work with him directly during their playing days offer him respect, but it is often grudging. He never really became as much a part of the establishment as he should have been.

The reason? Most probably because Wenger took the English game and turned it on its head. Broccoli replaced beer, stretching became more important than standing and listening. Science. Video evidence informed strategy. Keep the ball. Don't hit it long. That meant transforming pitches too. In soccer Wenger proved that data works, but many at the heart of the game deny that. This book will help us to understand why.

The History of Analytics

'I don't believe skill was, or ever will be, the result of coaches. It is a result of a love affair between the child and the ball.' – Roy Keane – ex Manchester United and Republic of Ireland 'hard-man' midfielder.

The 2012 Champions League final looked a bit of an oddity from the start. The biggest club game certainly in Europe, and probably the world (although not the richest – there's a great quiz question for an end of season celebration...) would be played not at a neutral venue, not even home and away over two legs. No, this sporting drama would take place at the home stadium of one of the competitors.

The Allianz Arena is a splendid stadium, there can be no doubt about that. But as the home of Bayern Munich, who would be seeking to defeat Chelsea to lift the Champions League title, it threw a small but significant advantage to the German club. Still, since the venue for the final is decided well in advance, nothing could be done. Chelsea would also play the game without their iconic leader and outstanding center half, John Terry, who had kneed Barcelona's Chilean striker Alexis Sanchez off the ball during the semi final.

Although Bayern dominated the game, and took the lead, Didier Drogba equalized for the English club and the game drifted into penalties. Chelsea's only previous Champions League final had ended in defeat on penalties against Manchester United – that was four years previously – but this time they were as prepared as they could be. Petr Cech was their keeper, and he knew the favored position each of the Bayern players would take with their penalties.

'Cech guesses right again,' said a commentator during that shoot out. He was wrong. There was no guess work involved. The Chelsea back room team had gathered every piece of video footage they could (there was lots, even in 2012), researched every corner of soccer data to know where the Bayern players were likely to place their penalties. Remember also, this was a high-pressure situation. Psychologically, the best way to cope with such pressure is to follow normal procedures. Do what you normally do. Muscle memory and all that.

Bayern did, and Cech applied his knowledge of each player to choose the right direction to dive on each occasion. The shoot-out went to sudden death, with six penalties taken by each team. Cech saved three, including the sudden death decider, and Chelsea won the

Champions League for the only time in their history. Data analysis in action.

Not, though, that it did much good for Chelsea's manager, Roberto Di Matteo. The Italian is famously pictured mouthing 'I did it,' to the London team's inscrutable Russian owner as he went to collect his medal. Roman Abramovich stares back expressionlessly, offering no more than a nod. No wild celebrations for him. Like many before and since, Di Matteo would be on his way a few weeks' later. Even winning the Champions League seems not good enough for the billionaire oligarch. (In fact, this was a pattern he was to repeat a number of times in the future. In 2015, in his second spell as Chelsea manager, Jose Mourinho was sacked just months after securing the Premier League title, Antonio Conte won the Premier League as well, but was on his way a year later, despite winning the FA Cup that season. Maurizio Sarri secured the Europa League cup in 2019 but had been replaced by the start of the following season. Whether Abramovich and his team employ analytics in sacking their managers is hard to say, but if so, they must apply different criteria to most.)

To return to Petr Cech, though, it was interesting to hear what he had to say afterwards. 'Six penalties the right way and I saved three, so basically the homework was very good.' To pick on the fact that he – along with the goalkeeping staff and data scientists at the club – had employed analytics to work out where the Bayern penalty takers were most likely to place their kicks indicates that this was a field that was still not commonplace in the game.

So, what is the history of analytics in soccer? Perhaps a good place to start involves another big match, another English footballing side and another penalty. It is 1990. Italy. The World Cup. England have reached the quarter finals and their opponents are the highly unpredictable but dangerous African team, Cameroon with their aging but iconic striker, Roger Milla to the fore. Milla had scored twice in extra time to secure the African nation victory over Columbia in the last sixteen, while a late goal (also in extra time) had given England victory over Belgium.

England won, equalizing with a late goal from their striker and now TV presenter Gary Lineker, before the forward scored again to win the game in extra time. Both of his goals were penalties. The first was crucial; miss it and Cameroon would almost certainly be the ones to progress to the semi finals, so close to the end of the game was the kick awarded.

Lineker sent the goalkeeper the wrong way. But it was not by chance that he did so. The previous day he had been about to take a few practice penalties during England's short time training in the quarter final stadium. The much-loved England manager, Bobby Robson, received a message. Apparently, somehow, a member of the Cameroon camp had gained access to the stadium and was now watching the England team train. Robson sent a message to Lineker – 'Put the ball to the opposite side to your favored one.' Nothing more. Lineker got the message, but only later understood why it had been sent. But he did as he was told. The Cameroon spy reported back to his goalkeeper, telling him the England penalty taker's favored side. Which was, of course, wrong.

Come the match itself, the keeper followed the guidance he had been given, and Lineker placed the ball to where he normally did – the opposite corner. Early use of analytics in soccer? Maybe.

Eight years later and data analysis was becoming more widespread. But not especially effective. Studies of the world cup in France in 1998 demonstrated that most goals were scored after minimal passes. Technical directors across the world considered the implications and decided to promote the kind of long ball game which damages technical skills (it becomes a physical battle where speed and size win over skill) and diminishes the spectacle soccer offers. Long ball teams are soon found out, and rarely succeed.

We can head back further. In the English game, during the late 1960s and early 1970s, Leeds United were the most powerful force. Their manager, the hard-nosed Don Revie, famously produced detailed dossiers on every aspect of opponent's play. Their strengths and weaknesses. Such early data analysis was simplistic, lacked objectivity and could go crushingly wrong if the scout attending opponents' matches allowed his own opinions to colour the facts of the game. But nevertheless, this sort of dossier building was not unknwon, and there can be little doubt that Revie's tactics were not unique to him (although they were not commonplace). This kind of relatively primitive data analysis was already happening more than sixty years ago. As we shall see later, perhaps even more than this. Anything to gain an advantage.

However, it was the turn of the millennium and the emergence of 'Moneyball' which really saw data analytics take hold. There can be little doubt that two other factors played a big part in the emergence of data analytics as a key component of the modern game as well. Firstly, was the rise in efficiency of technology, secondly the rapid growth in the screening of matches through television, especially Sky TV.

Let us consider these three aspects in turn.

Moneyball, for those unfamiliar with the term, was scheme of Billy Beane, the General Manager of Oakland Athletics baseball team. Oaklands were not a great side. Not even a very good one when Beane took over. In fact, to refer to the Californians as distinctly average would be overstating their record.

But Beane had the foresight to look outside the box in order to promote his team's success. He called on the work of a man called Bill

James, and by analyzing the metrics of players he found ways to make his collection of journeyman players into champions. New tactics emerged from the data analysis that he completed, it was used in-game to change the course of a match and players found their own niches to exploit. The combined result was the group of workaday players at Oaklands embarked on one of the longest winning streaks in baseball history.

Wise owners and wiser coaches in soccer opened their eyes to what was happening in other sports – something we take for granted today but was still considered revolutionary as recently as twenty years ago – and applied the methodology of Beane to their own sport. The use of analytics was not unheard of in soccer back then, as we have seen, but suddenly it was to move from the shadows to the forefront of the game.

But soccer is not baseball. Baseball, like other bat and ball games, is relatively easy to analyze, to break down into constituent parts. Just consider the stats fans of the game, how much ready information they have – and have had – in enjoying their take on the sport. Soccer is different. It is much more fluid as a sport. Advantage changes in the blink of an eye. The only aspects of the game relatively easy to gather data upon are the set pieces, penalties, free kicks, corners.

This is evidenced through a simple glance at the behavior of fans (we hope that by the time you are reading this book, supporters will be allowed back into stadia across the world!). Consider the excitement when a corner is won. Crowd noise increases, hearts beat faster, superstitions are followed…both for the attacking side and the defense. But in fact, statistically, a corner is a relatively benign advantage to win. The chances of a goal being scored is remote, and indeed there is a risk that a corner opens the offensive side up to a counterattack. We will come back to this point later.

The game is so fluid that to analyze it in the sort of depth that would bring about serious advantage requires effective technology. And, to maximize this on the training ground, mobile technology. The first 'tablets' might have been around in the 1990s, but their use was limited, their cost prohibitive and as a tool, they worked better as a science fiction prop than a data analysis device. Microsoft released their Tablet PC in 2002, and the iPad only arrived on the scene in 2010. The first smartphone, incredibly, hit the market in 1992 but was not especially smart. Again, it the first decade of the 21st century before such technology becomes sufficiently available and advanced to offer benefit in analytics.

So, early analytics even in this century could offer only limited benefit to soccer coaches. It is understandable, therefore, that it was not widely used. In fact, the data organization Opta started collecting data from matches for the relatively new English Premier League in 1996 (the year, incidentally, that Arsene Wenger, mentioned in the introduction, took over at the club where he became a household name, Arsenal.) The collection of stats was what we might call a tad nerdy. Passes, tackles, the distance players travelled, shots and so forth. 'Big' Sam Allardyce got into analytics because he was seeking a way, the story has it, to match the big clubs' achievements despite the small budget Bolton Wanderers had to operate. Statisticians cost a lot less than players, so he invested in them. The direct style associated with his teams came from the fact that his statisticians worked out that the ball changed hands (or feet) around four hundred times in an average game, and if the ball could be won and shifted forward quickly an exposed defense were more likely to give away a set piece – throw in, corner or even better, free kick. His data analysts deduced that 30% of goals at this time were being scored as a result of set plays, and so Allardyce focused on this area of the game, actually creating the situation where his team scored half their goals from dead ball situations.

But another problem existed. To find out about a player a side might consider buying, or the tactics employed by an opposing team with whom a side had a fixture coming up meant sending a scout to watch a game. As skilled as these people might be, they could only gather what they saw, and what they remembered. Simply, details would be sketchy. And often tinted through the lenses with which the scouts observed them. Scouts have been employed for decades, depending on the wealth of the club sending them out more or less information could be gathered by them. But the benefits they could bring were highly limited.

What was needed was a database of detailed information. The sort that led to the two-hour video of every Bayern Munich players' penalties for the previous five years which Petr Cech had studied with his coaches. That sort of video record could only emerge with the increase in TV coverage. No longer would teams have to rely on recording (at least, when video recorders became available – 1963, surprisingly) brief highlights of selected matches to study in depth, but just about any important game would be available.

Need a striker? Hours of the players' performances would immediately be available. And soon, as analytics improved, became more popular and more available, the range of data coaches could access would accelerate beyond imagination.

There were bumps on the journey. In 2010 John Henry, an American, purchased Liverpool Football Club. Once the giants of Europe, Liverpool were still a major team, one of the world's richest. But it seemed as though their real glory days were behind them. Henry, though, thought he could change that. He owned Boston Red Sox and had employed the Moneyball style data analysis used by Beane at Oaklands to enable his own baseball team to win the World Series. That was in 2004 and represented the Red Sox's first World Series win for the best part of a century (86 years, to be precise.) Surely, believed Henry, he could use the same analytics to bring back the glory days to his football team.

A great example of how this might emerge quickly arose. The Liverpool Director of Football, Damien Comoli (incidentally, a friend of Moneyball's Billy Beane) identified that Liverpool possessed statistically two of the best passers in the league in Steward Downing and Jordan Henderson. What they needed to bring success was to marry these players' passing talents with a striker who could convert the chances they made. They settled on the traditional, old fashioned number nine, Andy Carroll.

Immediately, the problem of marrying statistics without an expert knowledge of football showed itself. Yes, Carroll was a real threat from crosses. And yes, Henderson and Downing were good passers. But such statistics on their own do not tell the entire story. Henderson and Downing's passing was accurate, but rarely incisive. Carroll was good in the air, but few goals are scored from crosses.

Whilst Liverpool were to be admired for trying to apply analytics to improve their results, it was clear that simply using data was not enough. The *right* data was needed. Comoli paid for his errors with his job; as a striker, Andy Carroll has never recovered. He will not be familiar to any soccer fan who does not hold a high interest in the English Premier league.

There is a saying in the English game that a player or team is only going to succeed if they 'can produce their best on a cold, windy night in Stoke.' The cliché could easily belong in our list presented in the introduction to this book and is sadly out of date now. For those not familiar, Stoke is a tough Midlands city in the industrial heartlands of the UK, and can lay claim to a number of unwelcome boasts. At various times, for example, it has been home (if that is the word) to Britain's least expensive house, and also its biggest crime rates.

Tony Pulis was coach of Stoke City during much of its long stay in the Premier League. Nowadays, at least of the time of writing, it has plunged out of the top division and looks unlikely to return for a while, but in Pulis' heyday, to travel to Stoke for an evening game in winter was considered the biggest challenge in English soccer. In fact, the stats do not back this up, but nevertheless Stoke's claustrophobic Britannia Stadium could be intimidating. Pulis had in his time a fairly unremarkable full back called Rory Delap. Delap was a good professional, just about Premier League class, but he did have one remarkable talent. He could throw the ball like a bullet, with considerable accuracy, velocity and a very flat trajectory. Pulis examined the data and understood that a throw in from Delap was more dangerous than a corner, if Stoke could win the throw in an attacking position. The data backed this up, and it was particularly effective at home, when the Stoke fans would take the roof off the stadium with their intimidating noise every time a throw in was awarded.

It did not matter who won the first touch, the ensuring chaos from a Rory Delap throw caused desperation in the opposing defenses, and reduced confidence to the thinnest thread. Thus, Stoke played a fast game, getting the ball forward quickly and into the channels, forcing defenses to play the ball out for throw ins. In examining Stoke's long throw tactics, we have an example of how the development of analytics can make a real impact on a team, but only when other conditions – player skill set, reputation, crowd and so forth – also enhance the tactic.

And so, it goes on. As technology improves, so do the metrics available. But, as we saw with the Liverpool example above, only when that data is used wisely, can it make a real difference. The growth of analytics has revolutionised soccer. But it hasn't changed it completely.

WHAT MAKES A WINNER?

Can the poverty gap be overcome in soccer?

'The secret is to believe in your dreams; in your potential that you can be like your star, keep searching, keep believing and don't lose faith in yourself.' – Neymar Jr.

Neymar is a fine player, but his explanation of finding success might be seen as a tad romantic. A touch simplistic. Please forgive a moment's cynicism. Money would be the obvious and fairly simplistic answer to the chapter title question. 'There is a clear correlation between spend on wages and league position' wrote the Planet Football online magazine at the beginning of the 2017 season. In the season just finished (2019-2020), the top six biggest spenders of transfer fees occupied the five of the top six positions in the English Premier league. The only intruders were the hardly small-town club Chelsea, whose eighth biggest spend delivered a third-place finish, and qualification for the Champions League. Tottenham, the only one of the top six spenders to miss out on a top six finish were seventh.

But is that a purely English phenomenon? After all, the Premier League is the richest in the world, with its lucrative TV contracts delivering wealth to the elite in previously unimaginable quantities. Top teams in the Spanish, German and, previously, Italian leagues might out perform English teams in Europe, but whereas there are possibly eight English sides who can reasonably be expected to challenge for top honours – the Manchester clubs, Liverpool and Everton, Chelsea, Arsenal and Spurs as well as, recently, Leicester City – in Germany there are only really two: Bayern Munich and Dortmund; in Spain perhaps three – Barcelona, Real Madrid and Atletico Madrid. (Maybe, owing to their fine recent Europa League exploits, Sevilla could just squeeze in as a fourth Spanish side.) In Italy with the demise of the Milan empire, only Juventus might be considered a truly top European side these days.

So, how close is the actual transfer budget of the biggest clubs to their actual rankings across the continent? Taking the decade up to and including the summer transfer window of 2019, here are the top twelve net spenders, and what that has delivered in terms of trophies and Champions League qualifications.

Liverpool came in twelfth; their return up until that time being a Champions League trophy and four five Champions' league qualifications. Bayern Munich were eleventh, and their outlay seems to have delivered a good return although the fact that their only consistently serious opposition has been Dortmund over that period might explain the mismatch between titles and spend. And so, it continues.

- 12th Liverpool (£297million)
- 11th Bayern Munich (£328 million)
- 10th Inter Milan (£333 million)
- 9th Real Madrid (£397 million)
- 8th Arsenal (£413 million)
- 7th Juventus (£421 million)
- 6th Chelsea (£422 million)
- 5th AC Milan (£436 million)
- 4th Barcelona (£562 million)
- 3rd Manchester United (£847 million)
- 2nd Paris St Germain (£847 million)
- 1st Manchester City (£1.1 billion)

So, the biggest net spenders have been Manchester City, second biggest Paris St Germain and third in the open wallet league Manchester United.

But it is here that maybe we begin to see some inconsistencies in the balance between spend and reward. If the Champions League is taken as the gold standard of European success then surely, if the relationship between spend and trophies is absolute, these three teams would have dominated European competition in that period. They haven't. In the ten years between 2010 and 2019 their Champions League record has been thus, combined: no titles, one final

(Manchester United, in 2010) and two semi-finals, the first being on Manchester United's route to the final, the only other one from Manchester City halfway through the decade. Paris St Germain did reach the final in 2020, but that comes just after the period of our assessment.

In fact, semi-finals and onwards have been dominated by the three Spanish giants of Real Madrid (9th biggest net spenders), Barcelona (4th) and Atletico Madrid (outside top 25) and Bayern Munich (11th). There have been good showings by Liverpool (12th) and Juventus (7th).

The link, though, does not always prove to be exact, as we can see if we dig deeper still. Let us take the English Premier League in the 2015-2016 season. This was of course the year when 5000-1 outsiders Leicester City won the title. The big spenders that season were, in order, Manchester City (just for a change!) with £154.4 million spent, the other Manchester club, United, with £115.3 million paid out on new players, Liverpool with £93.1 million and Chelsea, with a relatively, for them, moderate outlay of £76.8 million. Respectively, these teams finished 4th, 5th, 8th and 10th. The fifth highest that season were Newcastle United, who laid out just half a million pounds less than Chelsea. Their reward? Relegation.

The champions Leicester came in a lower mid table slot with a moderate spend of £36.6 million; Tottenham Hotspurs spent more, their eighth place £53.3 million outlay on new players delivering a plus five league position of third. But the team who really upset the theory that spend equates to success were Arsenal. The North London side achieving a second-place league finish (which included, incidentally, beating the eventual champions both home and away) with the lowest spend in the division.

Our conclusion so far would seem to suggest that money makes a big difference to the fortunes of a professional soccer team yet is not the overriding factor. But before we try to identify what that factor might be and look at length at how analytics might help a coach, owner, director of football or whoever achieve their ultimate goal, perhaps we should consider whether our look the somewhat blunt statistic of net transfer spend is too simplistic.

Perhaps a better tool to use to relate money spent with team success is a side's wage bill. Top of the tree is perhaps Europe's most successful side over the past twenty years, Barcelona. £453 million is their annual outlay in keeping their players in Ferraris and Rolex watches.

Second come Real Madrid, who spend £369 million a year ensuring that their well-paid superstars can afford the latest haircuts.

- 3rd Paris St Germain (£289 million) – dominant domestically, but just one European final in the last decade, that in the Covid struck season just past.
- 4th Manchester United (£286 million). The highest wage bill in the Premier League just about delivering Champions League football.
- 5th Bayern Munich (£270) – probably Europe's best side at present, and (at the time of writing) European champions.
- 6th Manchester City – (£267 million). Dominant, with Liverpool, domestically but only the most minor of English trophies for the money.
- 7th Liverpool (£255 million). Seems a bargain for a domestic league title and European Champions League title in the last two seasons.
- 8th Chelsea (£236 million) to squeeze into Champions League qualification.
- 9th Arsenal (£232 million). A coach who did not work out with the club, Unai Emery, makes that figure look expensive, but his replacement, Mikel Arteta, delivering two domestic trophies in six months, suddenly makes the spend seem worthwhile.
- 10th Juventus (£224 million). Delivered domestic dominance.
- 11th Atletico Madrid (£182 million). Again, a relatively modest outlay for the returns achieved over the past few seasons.

- 12th Borussia Dortmund (£160 million). A way behind Bayern Munich domestically, but also a much smaller club.

The conclusion we must reach from this wage spend versus return is that, as with transfer spending, money makes a big difference, but it is not everything.

So, what is it that does equal up the very richest from the merely extremely wealthy? The answer, it would appear, is something that the coach can offer. Let us examine how much of this value-added benefit comes from the use of analytics. The 2019-2020 season is perhaps not a good example in that the long break from Covid offered an extensive mid-season break and, in some leagues, led to the curtailment of the season. Nevertheless, it is useful because it offers an insight into the squad depth needed to win titles even when that break unexpectedly arrives.

So, to take the French Ligue 1, Paris St Germain were, for the third consecutive season, champions. Just for extra icing on the cake, they also won the Coupe de France and the Coupe de la Ligue, and were, as we have seen, runners up in the Champions league. They played forty-nine games across all competitive competitions, which included winning the one off Trophee des Champions. Eleven rounds of their national league competition were cancelled due to Covid 19. In completing this successful season, they used no less than thirty-one players. In fact, the only member of the first team squad not used was the fourth-choice goalkeeper, Garissone Innocent. Most appearances came from their midfielder Angel di Maria. Twenty-one players made at least twenty appearances.

Thirty players made it on to the pitch for Juventus, with sixteen of them making at least twenty appearances, but move to England, and an astonishing forty-five players represented Liverpool as they became League and World Club Champions. However, more in keeping with other European teams who won their domestic title, they used sixteen players more than twenty times. Still, in a sign that the Liverpool team was settled, all but two of these made at least thirty-seven appearances.

The overall Liverpool total is a little skewed in that they were forced to field an almost completely third choice team in one League Cup round when the fixture clashed with their World Club Championship.

In winning the Bundesliga, Bayern Munich's use of players matched the pattern established above. Fourteen players with at least twenty appearances, and another fifteen appearing at least once.

What we can reasonably conclude is that the modern game is a squad game, one in which the most successful teams have a core of around sixteen to twenty players on whom they can call for most big matches, with a number of additional players – perhaps often youngsters being tested out – who come in for the smaller cup competitions. The days of a squad of thirteen or fourteen players taking a team through a domestic season are long gone.

Nevertheless, an interesting statistic is thrown up. Norwich City finished bottom of the Premier League in England. Yet only thirteen players made at least twenty appearances, and just ten more than twenty-five. Seventeen players made less than twenty appearances, overwhelmingly coming on as a substitute. Ten players made ten or fewer appearances. This points to a lack of squad depth in quality, if not quantity, which may well have been a major contributor to Norwich's demise.

So, if we conclude that in order to be successful a team needs a core squad of at least sixteen players who can perform consistently at the highest level, with a similar number who can come to replace injured players, or to offer squad rotation to give a player a rest, the question is begged, how are those players selected in the first place?

The answer is, of course, through analytics. Through study of data in determining which players might progress through a side's academy programme, and also which players will become transfer targets.

We have seen that it is vital to be a rich club to win the biggest competitions, but not necessarily the richest. These days, with their multi billionaire owners, Manchester City and Paris St Germain are among the top table (or, in their cases, the top top table) of the wealthiest teams in the world. Neither have won the Champions League. So, what else contributes to success in its highest form?

Tactics, team spirit, the luck (or preparation?) to avoid major injuries to key players. All clearly play their part. When Barcelona were the best team in the world, during the days of the great Spanish international side of the late noughties and into the beginning of the last decade, their players were all superb. There can be no denying that. But under the coaching of Pep Guardiola, they developed the tika taka style of play which revolutionised their tactical approach to controlling possession, and which analytics suggest no team were able to replicate.

Built up on rondo training sessions – weighted drills which enabled some but minimal pressure to be put on the ball, allowing players to develop the finest of touches – Barcelona moved the ball quickly and fluidly. Often playing with a false nine – in other words, no out and out centre forward – their possession-based play created opportunities for goals for players all over the park.

Of course, it helped that in the three greats of the team, Xavi, Iniesta and, of course, the imperious Lionel Messi, they had the players with the touch, insight and creativity to exploit their possession-based game. Nevertheless, it was a system of play mimicked across the world, even if never truly matched.

But, it seems, all tactical formations have their day. Perhaps opposing coaches manage to work out, through analytics, how to negate the tactics of Guardiola's men. And so, soccer evolves. Probably the most recent tactical trend has been the high press. First seen at the fast paced, all action, Borussia Dortmund side under the leadership of Jurgen Klopp, and then in his successful Liverpool team, this approach requires incredible teamwork and extreme fitness.

Out of possession, a team hunts the ball in packs, pressurising defenders who are, usually, less skilled on the ball than team mates who operate further up the park. By closing down teams close to their own goal, players are forced to either play the ball long, conceding possession or, more dangerously, try to play out, risking the loss of possession in their own half. The high pressing team, with players already well up the pitch for the press, then turn this transition point into rapid attack, outnumbering opponents in their own half and creating serious goal threats.

But already, coaches are finding ways to overcome this. A key approach which is being seen across major leagues over the world finds teams playing the ball out from the back. This requires intense training drills to create space and improve touch. But often the key is the spare player; and that is the goalkeeper. Nowadays, top goalkeepers are not just required to save the ball, but to be comfortable in possession, to be able to pass and, even, dribble, with confidence, accuracy and two feet. Of course, this has led to some farcical goals being conceded; keepers trying to beat an onrushing striker and being tackled; defenders mis-controlling a pass or hitting a wayward one of their own. But clearly coaches feel that this kind of building from the back is the way forward. Literally. Certainly, it has led to some splendid goals as opponents push on the high press and leave gaps in behind. The very opening game of the 2020 season in the English Premier League illustrated the point. A couple of short, simple passes starting with Bernd Leno, the keeper, led to the midfielder Mohammed Elneny breaking towards the halfway line. He slipped the ball into Alexander Lacazette on the halfway line, who was fouled as he turned. Willian picked up the loose ball, strode on for ten metres before launching an excellent cross field pass to striker Pierre Emerick Aubameyang. The speed of the break meant the deadly forward was left in acres of space (a nice football cliché, that, worthy of inclusion in the introduction). He broke inside from the left-hand channel, cutting the ball onto his right foot and the ball was suddenly nestling in the net.

A goal for 2020. Intuitive, yes. But we shall see, one built upon the back of complex and extensive analytics.

ANALYTICS IN ACTION

Case studies illustrating the effectiveness high quality analytics can deliver.

'From the beginning when something was wrong I've been saying: "Dilly Ding, dilly-don, wake up, wake up!" So on Christmas Day I bought for all the players and all the staff a little bell. It was just a joke.' – Claudio Ranieri, Leicester City manager when they did the impossible, and won the English Premier League.

Maybe it was Ranieri's generous gift to his staff that helped to secure Leicester City that 5000-1 Championship title. More likely, it was a little more complicated than that. To help us to understand the way effective use of analytics can really lead to the development of a soccer team, let us consider some detailed case studies. Later, we will take a look at Leicester, but to begin with, let us head to the German leagues.

TSG Hoffenheim

The German side are traditionally one from the lower rungs of football. Their extended stay in the top division of the Bundesliga is down, as much as anything else – in fact, probably more than anything else – to the influence of effective use of soccer analytics. TSG

Hoffenheim generate revenue of around 65 million euros per annum. That is equivalent to about $75 million. We have seen in earlier chapters that such income is not going to deliver Champions League success, or even a league title in such a competitive system as the German leagues. Therefore, that Hoffenheim have not only retained their top-level status but enhanced their stay in the top division represents considerable success for a small club.

TSG Hoffenheim, as it is today, was formed in 1945 when the local football and gymnastics clubs combined. Even as recently as the beginning of the 1990s, the side was amateur, and competing in the Baden-Wittenberg A- Liga. So, what? we might think. But Hoffenheim were actually taking part in the eighth division of that league. Well down the German soccer pyramid. However, improvement followed and by the mid-1990s they had reached the sixth tier of German football.

It was ten years later that the big push came, under the club's owner Dietmar Hopp, a computer software tycoon who had the vision to see that effective analysis could overcome the small size of the club. In the early days, technology was combined with a very comprehensive youth development programme and in-depth scouting. When the 2008 season began the fairy tale was almost delivered, and Hoffenheim were in the top division of the Bundesliga.

In 2015, Hopp took the next step, developing one of only three 'footbonauts' in the world. This is a training tool, based on analytics, which collected metrics on player skill and strength. The move was controversial, and in a pattern we will see repeated, 'soccer professionals' on the backroom staff were dubious about the use of technology, and resistant to change as a result.

But Hopp was determined, and the first area of improvement he sought was to make players' decision making faster and better. Jan Mayer was the sports psychologist at Hoffenheim – just a small village which is home to little more than 3000 inhabitants – charged with bringing about this change.

He discovered that footballers really were better in the modern game. For example, in comparing the 2014 World Cup with the 1966 tournament, research demonstrated that passing was 35% more accurate, and considerably quicker. Even in the relatively short period between 2006 and 2014, the German national team, using Hopp's own SAP's data analysis support system, had speeded up their game to shift the ball from an average of 2.9 seconds on a single player's possession, to 0.9 seconds. It is a much-repeated truism that the ball moves faster than a player, so the quicker that player can release the ball, the more damage will be inflicted on opponents.

Mayer discovered two kinds of thinking in players. The muscle memory, automatic decisions which are often wrongly called 'instinct'. This might include, for example, controlling a ball on the half turn ready to off load an effective pass, whilst protecting the ball with their body. Secondly, and this was the factor which advanced technically very good footballers into top class ones, 'executive function' decision making. This is, in simple terms, tactical thinking.

Mayer identified that if he could speed up this executive thinking, then players would become better. He achieved this through technology. One example was his development of a 180-degree Helix artificial environment, where avatars are displayed representing team mates and opponents. Fundamentally, Mayer and Sapp created a personalised video game which could adapt to players' strengths and weaknesses, quicken their responses and lead to problem solving scenarios.

'Video gaming, it turns out, is good for improving executive functions, parents might be sad to hear,' explained Mayer with a smile.

Indeed, the work led to players demonstrating improved positional awareness and their peripheral vision was enhanced.

This is just one of the analytical programmes Hoffenheim employs. Utilising Hopp's links to SAP, the club also uses a package called 'Sports One'. This contains software to measure the impact of team management and offer solutions for different scenarios. It includes programmes on team planning as well as the more traditional elements of player fitness and scouting.

But the key question is, does it work? The evidence would seem to suggest that it does. Hoffenheim are among the most prudent teams in the Bundesliga when it comes to spending. Whether that is due to necessity, or policy (or, more probably, both) is a question for the accountants. Nevertheless, the club constantly overachieves compared it pure economics (i.e., average attendance, spending on transfers, spending on wages.) It sits thirteenth in crowd numbers – even more remarkable considering the town itself is so small. It is mid table with regards to its wage bill and its transfer spend. Yet, last season once again achieved a top six finish, qualifying for European competition. Already, in the early stages of the 2020 2021 campaign, it is off to a flying start, topping the league after the first few games.

Remembering that the team is already performing vastly above its natural level by being in the top division of the Bundesliga, then its finishing position in the league prior to the introduction of SAP technology, that is, the period between 2008 and 2013 was 11th on average. In the six seasons since its introduction, that average position has risen to 7th. Even more crucially, in that period the club qualified twice for the Champions League. Imagine that, a club from a village of 3000 people, playing in one of the four most powerful leagues in the world, qualifying for the Champions League. Surely, that represents as much success as Real Madrid winning three Champions League finals in a row.

Leicester City – The Impossible Champions.

The end of the 2014/2015 season had not been good for Leicester City, lower mid table team from a rambling and, to be honest, fairly nondescript East Midlands conurbation. In fact, Leicester was more famous, in a sporting sense, for its rugby union team, the Tigers, one of the strongest in the country. Beyond that…well, Leicester is located close to the M1, England's main motorway and…umm…has a space museum and sewage works (adjacent, but not combined, fortunately) open to the public.

Then Nigel Pearson, a manager who had helped save the club from relegation, was sacked. It was a somewhat sordid event that led to his dismissal. Some players, including his son, had filmed themselves on a pre-season tour up to some insalubrious activities in a hotel bedroom with a group of local girls. They were not the first, nor the last, young men to behave badly. But soccer is in the public eye. Even a team such as Leicester City. Pearson went, and in his place was appointed the Tinkerman, the experienced and more successful than he is given credit for Italian, Claudio Ranieri. The Leicester supporters were underwhelmed. Every fan thinks their club is the dream destination of every international player, every top-drawer manager. Of course, they are not. Leicester's faithful thought they deserved an emerging name such as Jurgen Klopp; they got a man they thought was a has been, with very little in the 'has' drawer. They were wrong.

To describe Leicester City football club as an also ran is to underestimate their ambition. And the use of technology they have employed to deliver it. Prozone is the main supplier of metric systems to Premier League clubs. Way back in the early years of the century, former England manager Sam Allardyce kept his unfashionable Bolton team in the top division largely thanks to the data his advocacy of analytics delivered. Leicester were one of the teams who really bought into this.

At the time of their greatest triumph (not just a flash in the pan, they progressed well in the Champions League the following season, and appeared to be the main challengers to Liverpool and Manchester City in the 2019/2020 season, before falling away on the restart following the suspension of the season for Covid 19.

During their peak, Leicester employed the most advanced system Prozone possessed. Players wore monitors which ensured maximum fitness. These measured metrics ranging from distance covered, through sprints and other high intensity runs. Players fitness was also protected through the use of a device called OptimEye S5. This was a monitor worn at the top of the back. One of its main purposes is to monitor the risk of injury. The monitor is able to track player performance and compare it to a player's normal maximum workload. Players are far more likely to be injured when they have overworked than when fresh. Not only because their physical condition is weakened, but also because mentally they tire, and therefore are more likely to make ill-judged decisions.

Thus, even when a player is performing well, coaching staff are able to track when their performance is about to fall away, and when they are at risk of injury. Then, a player can be substituted, or supported with a tactical change, helping to preserve their fitness.

Another significant risk factor for injury is returning to full action too soon after recovery from another injury. The system also helps to track this, measuring a player's workload in training, and comparing it to their normal data when fit.

As with Hoffenheim's use of data, the system worked. Leicester's first team was, in all likelihood, only the eighth or ninth best in the league. It was famously inexpensive to put together. Yet, that first team was better than other club's second and third choice players. Leicester incurred by far the fewest injuries during that season. Only a quarter of the most injured side, and there were just eighteen injuries requiring a match to be missed throughout the entire squad for the whole season.

Some media put this down to luck. But it is not luck. It is science. Effective use of analytics delivering results.

Leicester's miracle season was not just built on keeping their team fit. Each player received a personalised pre match and post-match report from the club's tech team itemising statistics, drawing conclusions from that data and backing it up with match footage. This is taking Don Revie's fifty-year-old practice of producing dossiers for his team to the nth degree. Every teacher will explain that meeting the individual needs of a pupil, and pitching their learning at their own level, is the way to deliver maximum progress. It makes absolute sense for soccer players to be taught in the same way.

Data, for home matches at least, was immediately available. The analytics' team occupied a room in the club's King Power Stadium with a direct link to the home changing room so it could be utilised during the half time team talk. Such analytics were used to identify where players were winning or losing individual duels, where opposition chances were coming from. The information was immediately presented to the back-room team and manager, so that it could be used to change the game.

Of course, cynics will say that the best managers will spot such trends in any case. This is true, to a certain extent. But no single pair of eyes can view eleven players as technology can. Even what coaches witness is judged through the blemished eyes of a human and filtered through the inevitable moods and prejudices from which we all suffer. Data is cold, and objective. That is its strength.

A further tool was that every player's performance was objectively assessed in terms of metrics – speed, distance run, passes, tackles, shots, sprints, high intensity runs and so forth – and compared against their season's average. Thus, the manager had an objective assessment of which players were at the top of their game, which were slipping, who needed a rest and who needed encouragement. Dilly ding, dilly dong.

Metrics cannot replace man management, but they can really help to enhance it.

But there is one more important factor which helps to explain how Leicester have managed to sustain their success to a large extent. One of the biggest challenges to the use of data is cynicism – the old pro attitude we highlighted earlier, and from which Hoffenheim suffered when they tried to introduce analytics. That cynicism is understandable for former professionals who had no experience of the benefits it could bring. But every player wants to play, and play well, whatever the worst elements of fan bases and the media might suggest. Every player wants to extend their short career, keep the fun and excitement and money flowing for as long as possible. Analytics help to extend a player's career. They do so in two ways. They identify physical factors to ensure the player stays fit and thus increases the chances of experiencing career shortening injuries. They also help a player to track down turns in form, helping them to focus on areas needing improvement, and keeping them in their manager's thinking when it comes to team selection.

Leicester's astonishing achievement in winning the Premier League was remarkable. But, perhaps, not quite as surprising as it might first appear.

Casemiro of Real Madrid – Using Metrics to Identify the Player a Team Needs

Real Madrid won three Champions' League finals in a row from 2016 to 2018. In the 2017 final, it was not the superstar Ronaldo who was identified as the Spanish team's greatest threat by their opponents, Juventus' coach, Massimiliano Allegri. Certainly, Ronaldo scored twice in Real's 4-1 victory, but Allegri identified the Brazilian Casemiro as the man who held the key to ensuring Real's flowing football could flourish.

Casemiro is an example of how a coach can use metrics to find the key piece of his or her jigsaw. Under Rafa Benitez, Real were a fine side, but the new manager Zinedine Zidane, one of the new breed of world class soccer players who donned the tracksuit and match day jacket and tie to coach leading teams.

The Real team that Zidane inherited glistened with diamonds. Luca Modric, Toni Kroos, Karim Benzima, Gareth Bale – all superstars in their own right and capable of more than adding lustre to the main jewel in the crown, the Portuguese giant Ronaldo. But while diamonds are brilliant in the right light, sometimes they can be dropped, and scatter. In tournaments as competitive as the Champions League and La Liga, mistakes are costly. Zidane identified that something was needed to hold the diamonds together, to keep them secure in the event that they did hit the floor.

That player would be a defensive midfielder. One who was reliable and disciplined and could be trusted to allow the jewels in front of him to glisten. Casemiro will frequently cover more than 13 kilometres during a match. A phenomenal amount, allowing him to adopt positions to both support attacks but also cover breaks by the opposition.

But Zidane needed more than just a stopper. The Real game plan was built on full backs getting forward, central midfielders pushing on to create a high press and winning possession to launch rapid attacks. What is therefore needed is a player who can pick up possession in deep midfield and launch accurate passes to begin new attacks at speed and with precision. Metrics on Casemiro indicated that he was among the best in Zidane's expensive squad in this role. Note, although he is more than capable of producing long range incisive passing, the sort that catches the eye, Casemiro is astonishingly accurate with his short passing game. His decision making is quick, and he passes with precision. He was also the best player in the squad to act as the pivot between defense and offense, his accurate passing and vision (identified, statistically, through his metrics) meant he could launch new attacks and allow his midfield colleagues to push on.

An issue with the attacking game Zidane wished to play was that, when an attack breaks down, any team is liable to an opponents' break. Despite their wealth and reputation, Real under Zidane were not immune to this. What was needed to mitigate this risk was a mobile and fit player – Casemiro – but also one with excellent positional discipline. Heat maps of the Brazilian's movement during the game showed a player who could be relied upon to be in the right place if an attack broke down.

When Zidane took over for the first time at Real Madrid, he took on a team which glistened like a sports car and was as fast and deadly. Only, while its engine was good, it was not a Rolls Royce. He needed a key component to get the absolutely best out of his splendid vehicle. As he once said, it was not another coating of gold paint that Real needed, as much as that might impress the crowd and the President, it was something to make the team reliable.

Through his study of the club's metrics, Zidane realised he had the very player already in his squad, albeit one lounging for the most part on the bench, or in the reserves. Casemiro was promoted to becoming the first name on the team sheet. He became the lynchpin around which the team could shine.

EMPLOYING ANALYTICS IN TRAINING

Building on our study of Leicester City's use of analytics in training, more analysis of the benefits metrics offer in training.

'How much soccer training is needed to become a top player? It depends on the efficiency of your training regime.' – Pele, the world's greatest ever player.

In this chapter we will delve even more deeply into looking at how analytics are used in the professional game in training sessions, and how that then translates into match strategy. As always, coaches of amateur and youth teams can take the examples of what is done at the pinnacle of the game and look to adapt this for their own circumstances.

The fact cannot be avoided that soccer as a sport contains more random plays than almost any other. The variables are immense and so using an objective process such as analytics will never solve every conundrum. But then, that is the joy of the game. If there were no random elements, results would be far more predictable. With a completely level playing field of objective data, the richest would always win, rather than just usually win as is the case at the moment.

This randomness of soccer is something we will consider in more detail later.

Nevertheless, soccer is not a sport determined by luck alone. Analytics can make a difference, and especially in training to get the most out of players, determine their fitness and give insights into their form. Analytics can be used to identify those areas of a players' game which need to improve, both for them to maximise their role in the team, but also to maximise their own potential.

At the very highest levels, players will be subject to intense metrics during their training sessions. Players wear GPS trackers to measure their movement, on and off the ball. Software is then used to translate the information to assess their work rate, movement, involvement and just about any other playing factor which might influence performance.

That is not all. Heart rate monitors will analyse fitness levels and help to optimise preparation for matches. Acceleration sensors will monitor the probably more useful analysis of movement which measures sprints and intense bursts of action. Such is the value to clubs of knowing their players' fitness levels that other, quite intrusive elements of tracking are beginning to emerge. Monitoring of diet is perhaps understandable. However, factors such as sleeping habits might help to promote performance, but one wonders quite where it will stop as clubs seek to get the optimum performance from their players.

The days of fish and chips plus a couple of pints of best beer on the way home from a game are long gone.

Indeed, the next stage of data analysis is beginning to emerge. Now there is so much data available that clubs have an excess of information. The stage analytics is now entering is looking at how the data is used; not just what data is employed. Basic data – distance run, tackles made, passes completed and so forth is simply not enough for clubs seeking to take a competitive advantage over their opponents.

The devil is in the details; never has the cliché been more appropriate. If soccer is about winning games, and surely at the professional level that is what it has become, then that is achieved by scoring more goals than one's opponents. Rarely these days are the commonplace hammerings that used to occur in International qualifying competitions seen. That is because it is easier to stop a team from scoring, than to score oneself. So, the 8-1 thrashing the likes of San Marino, or Liechtenstein, might have endured are rare. Instead, defeats are 2-0 or 3-0. Not really competitive, but on the road. (Liechtenstein is a good example, in their European Championship qualifying record, they have played 68 games, winning five and losing 54. They have scored twenty and conceded 190 goals in that time. But four of those wins and sixteen of their goals scored have been achieved in the last four tournaments. At the same time, they conceded an average of almost four goals a game before 2008, and just three goals a game since then.)

Thus, teams can now set up to defend and avoid defeat effectively. It is the drills employed in training which help them to develop efficience defensive strategies. Many do, hoping to score from a break, a defensive error from their stronger opponents or from a set play. Gaining that marginal 1% advantage from the innovative, original use of analytics might be enough to win a match against such a determined defense.

And so, analytics are employed in every aspect of a club. From youth development, through first team training, match strategy and tactics, post-match analysis, diet, sleep, transfer policy and up to direction from the board room.

Such demand creates both pressure and opportunity for the commercial analysts seeking business from clubs. To take Prozone once more, they constantly respond to the demands of clubs. One of their more recent innovations is a package called Performance Lab. This uses that pure data gathered during matches and training to offer strategic ideas on such diverse aspects of the game as Game Intelligence, Player monitoring, Asset Management and Tactical

Profiling. Old school managers might begin to wonder where their role will be in a few years' time. But the data makes a difference. The metrics, those aspects of data, make a difference. The information provided is used to inform the effectiveness of playing styles, assessing how well players buy into the tactics they are given.

It is used to quantify the ability of a player. It helps to reduce the risk of injury and measure the relative creativity of a soccer player.

And, reassuringly, even the analysts themselves recognise that their role is to support the coach, not replace him or her. At the end of the day, a moment of magic, a defensive error or a refereeing decision can often determine the outcome of a game. And analytics cannot predict those. Can they?

THE KEY METRICS FOR POST ANALYSIS

Building on our study of Leicester City's use of analytics in training, more analysis of the benefits metrics offer in training.

'It is better to win ten time 1-0 than to win once 10-0.' Vahid Halilhodzic, manager of the Morroco national team.

To find the true birth of analytics in soccer we can head back to the 1950s, and former RAF Wing Commander Charles Reep. Significantly, a soccer man as a fan only, not a player. His interest was in examining passing moves which led to goals. He discovered that most goals came after three or less passes.

The long ball game. Oh dear. We shifted forward to the late 1990s, and the emergence of Prozone, whose increasingly significant role in the game began with a previously successful club now lying a little in the doldrums – Derby County of the English championship.

Next, we skip a generation of players, and emerge into the previous decade. Slowly, it is dawning on coaches that simply knowing that David Silva scores just under a goal ever five games, and has a shooting accuracy of 34% is all very interesting, but offers little of the true story of the Spanish genius. Something more was needed.

Analytics companies sat up, sniffed the air and smelt the grass flavoured coffee. It was time to change in the world of analytics.

It is generally accepted today that there are two main ways to gather data; the first, long standing method, involves collecting aggregated data, and the other tracks real time movement of both players and the ball during the game. But whichever system is employed, there are certain key aims to ascertain. These are:

1) The extent to which the team were able to deliver the strategy and tactics planned for prior to the game.
2) The relative strength and performances of the opposition, and how that impacted on the delivery of the game plan.
3) The performances of individuals, including their ability to change plans as the need arose.

The analysis will then consist of quantitative judgements, that is the statistical and numerical data that is relevant to the game. This may include, for example, the amount of possession the team had, the amount of shots taken, those on target, those shots allowed by the coach's own defense. The kind of pure data that, with the technology now available, is relatively easy to assimilate. To be fair, such analysis has always taken place after games. It is just that now the data is accurate, rather than determined by the perception of those gathering the information.

The second part of the analysis is the more difficult to ascertain, and also more valuable. This is the new data noted at the outset of this chapter. That is the qualitative assessment of the game through a technical and tactical analysis of phases of the game.

An assessment that uses advanced technology to track movement of players on and off the ball, to capture phases of play and to assess how well players make decisions to anticipate what will happen next. This data not only tells a coach what their team, and the players who constitute it, achieved, but how they did so.

With these two sets of information available to the coach, he or she can now carry out their post match assessment of the game. For ease of description we will refer to the 'home' team as Team H, and the opposition as Team O as we explore how coaches might carry out their analysis.

Was the Strategy Delivered?

It is a reasonable place to begin. If the data demonstrates that the strategy was delivered, and the result was still poor, then the fault cannot lay with the players. Rather that the tactics were inadequate. The analytics used to determine the degree to which the coach's strategy was delivered will depend on what that strategy involved. For example, let's say that analysis of Team O identified a tendency for their full backs to advance. Is the strategy employed to counter this to get Team H's wide midfielders in an advanced position? Qualitative assessment might demonstrate that Team O's full backs did get forward, and quantitative assessment will show that they succeeded in ultimately creating five goal scoring opportunities, two of which were converted.

Qualitive assessment can then be used to identify why the wide midfielders in Team H found themselves retreating. This will be achieved by using video footage to examine the play motifs which led to Team O's full backs getting forward. Could it have been that Team H's full backs were drawn out of position, and this meant that the wide midfielders had to get back to cover?

Why did that occur? And so the complex puzzle heads towards a solution.

We can demonstrate how qualitative and quantitative data on the game can be used to analyse how this tactical advantage was secured by Team O, and how Team H can then work on this in their own training sessions to ensure it does not happen again. We should remember that every club in the league is employing similar levels of analytics, and if a weakness has been spotted in the way a team is set up, or how it operates tactically through a game, we can sure other will look to exploit this. It is vital if the coach wishes to keep his or her job that they respond quickly to the problem. We can see how they may do this through a series of bullet points as they use post match metrics' information.

1. Assessment of opposition Team O demonstrates that they create many goal scoring opportunities by pushing their full backs into advanced positions.

2. Measure to counter this is for Team H to keep wide midfielders advanced, forcing those full backs to prioritise their defensive rather than offensive duties.

3. Team H wide midfielders increasingly forced to track full backs from the 11th minute onwards.

4. Result was five goalscoring chances, and two goals conceded, leading to a 2-2 draw rather than victory.

5. Wide midfielders forced to track back to compensate for Team H full backs forced infield. The infield position was to cope with central striker and rapidly advancing central midfielder from Team O.

6. Qualitative assessment data shows this happened when Team H central defensive midfielder advanced too far with the ball, and the Team H attack subsequently broke down.

7. In this situation Team H central defense was forced into a 2 v 2 situation unless full backs tucked in.

8. When Team H full backs tucked in, Team O full backs broke forward at speed.

9. In order to prevent this, Team H wide midfielders adopted a deeper position than tactics prescribed.

10. This allowed Team O full backs to move increasingly forward as the game progressed.

11. Tactical challenge for training;: **central defensive midfielder to hold a more defensive position.**

12. Better movement from advanced players to give him earlier passing options.

Thus, the combination of quantitative and qualitative date is used to identify a tactical failing, leading to the opportunity for it to be addressed.

Moving on to the opposition, most coaches will determine their own tactics based on the relative style of their opponents. This is much more likely to figure in a coach's strategic planning if the opposition appears to be a stronger team. The extent to which managers and coaches do this does vary. The great Brian Clough was a coach who achieved astonishing levels of success with medium ranked teams – his Nottingham Forest side even won the European Cup – twice. He was notorious for setting his side out to play in the free style he favoured and trust them to outperform the opposition. Arsene Wenger features widely in this book; he too apparently spent relatively little time worrying about the opposition. Former players talk about training sessions being about their own game, not neutralising the tactics of their opponents. It is interesting to note that as financial constraints caused by building a new stadium impacted on player recruitment, his players were less able to react to the opposition than their predecessors during the clubs hayday. Commentators and pundits often put this down to 'lack of leadership' or 'absence of toughness'. It wasn't. Simply, Wenger's trust that his players could adapt to their opponents' play was less often delivered, because there were more lower level players on the pitch.

The highly successful Jose Mourinho, by contrast, is closely focussed on reducing the impact of an opponent, as were the defensively minded Tony Pulis and Sam Allardyce. Atletico's over achieving manager Diego Simeone is similarly pragmatic in the way he sets up his teams. Managing relatively weaker teams all three coaches pay much attention to being highly organised in defense and seeking a set piece opportunity to score. Burnley, achieving well under Sean Dyche, operate in a similar way.

Coaches will have examined in detail the tactics employed by the opposition and set their stall out accordingly. This will have included analysis of almost every aspect of a game. For example, how do the team approach corner and other set pieces? Do they man mark or zonal mark when defending? Do they favour the long ball, switching it forward quickly. How do they begin distributions from the goalkeeper?

Having reached conclusions on these points prior to the game, and set up tactics to counter these, coaches will examine the extent to which their opponents adhered to the plan as they consider their post match data. After all, if their opposition deviated strongly, that could be a sign that they felt the need to change tactics. If the opposition's tactical change worked, then that tells a story, perhaps about the inflexibility of the coach's own tactics. If not, then that is a positive.

How Did the Opposition Perform

The success of Team H can only be determined in relation to the performance of Team O. If, for example, Team O are usually relatively fixed in their positioning, running an average of say 9.2 kilometres per match, but against Team H they upped this to 9.7 kilometres, that would inevitably have an impact on the progression of the match.

Similarly, if a team always sets up in a 4-3-3 formation, that could well have impacted on Team H's strategy. When they shift to a 5-4-1 formation, which switches to 3-4-3 when in possession it would be Team H's ability to respond to this strategic change that will determine the success of the side. Again, mostly qualitative data would be employed to assess this, measuring as it does the progression of the game.

Individual Players

There is an undoubted pleasure in watching a game, as a fan, that is, and then reading its report in the papers the following day. Journalists love nothing more than evaluating each player's performance out of ten. Comparing that to our own judgement (neither of which are particularly objective) can be great fun.

Coaches need a much more analytical approach to assessing the performance of their individual players. The sorts of metrics they will consider include quantitative details such as:

- Shots
- Tackles
- Passes – short and long, plus the success rate of these.
- Distance run
- Sprints
- Sustained sprints
- Touches
- Dribbles
- Crosses
- Heat maps (which show a player's positional distribution during the game)

However, such pure but blunt data offers only a small part of a player's performance. Qualitative data is required to ascertain the success of these aspects of his or her game. For example, a player who

69

achieves a 96% pass rate, but nearly all of these are lateral or backwards, not made under pressure and create no scoring opportunities is less effective than a player with a 70% success rate, but who includes four key passes during the game.

Coaches will also have data from training and will be able to assess each players' impact compared to their optimum expectations.

Coaches are often accused of being non-committal in their post-match interviews, of uttering bland statements and failing to do more than protect their players. Irrespective of the fact that it will hardly help team spirit if a coach comes out and finds a scapegoat among their players for a disappointing result, the fact is that they probably do not have access to the full analytical breakdown of the match so quickly after the game. Even if their in house team has managed to produce something, in the short period between the end of the game and the interview they will not have had time to assess the findings properly, and it is right and proper that those findings should be shared with their team and fellow coaches before the public as a whole.

Indeed, clubs guard their analytics like they are soccer's crown jewels. They will keep not only the individual data secret, especially the complex qualitative assessments, but also how their analysts reached the conclusions which they found.

Analytics have become as guarded as the team sheet, only to be shared when no other option remains.

USING ANALYTICS TO SATISFY SQUAD REQUIREMENTS

How analytics can be used as a team develops

'Luck has nothing to do with success.' – Diego Maradona

Red Star Belgrade might no longer be in the very top drawer of European soccer, but they are not far below it. The Serbian team are the only club from that country, or prior to that, Yugoslavia, to have won the European Cup. They achieved this impressive feat back in 1991. Domestically, they are highly dominant, having won their national championship thirty-one times, and their main home cup competition no less than on twenty-four occasions.

Case Study – Lorenzo Ebecilio

A couple of years ago the club identified the need to improve their offensive strengths with the addition of another attacking midfielder. Like most officials charged with recruitment would traditionally do, they began to scan their own leagues, then further afield, using their network of scouts to give insights on the sort of player they might find could fit their system and satisfy their needs.

Oddly enough, the league in the small island of Cyprus was not one that they considered. After all, it was a reasonable conclusion to reach that if any player there, or in one of the other small leagues that proliferate across the globe, was going to be good enough to make a difference to one of the stronger teams in Europe then that would already be known. Further, one of the really big clubs would have snapped him up.

It is a sign of the way analytics are growing that small businesses are springing up, there to widen the range of clubs who might be able to access information about promising but unknown players. That can only be a good thing for the game as a whole. We have already seen that money talks. But the further down the money tree that a voice can make itself heard, the more competitive the leagues – domestic and continental – will become. No longer will the likes of a small handful of super rich clubs – Barcelona, Bayern Munich, Real Madrid, Liverpool, Manchester United and City, Chelsea, Juventus and the Milan Teams, Paris St Germain to name most of them – win not because they are necessarily well run, or brilliantly coached. Instead, they succeed because their owners – or finance structures – simply allows them to go out and pay whatever is necessary for the handful of truly world class players available in the world. (That is not to say that these clubs are not well run…they are, which makes them stronger still).

The first result of this spread of high level data availability will be to open up competitions more to the second tier of top (but not top top) clubs – the likes of Olympiakos of Greece, Leicester City of England, Lyon in France and, of course, Red Star Belgrade. But more than this, there will be many players around the world who could, given the opportunity of a better structure and better team mates, move from the 'very good' category into that elite of the 'world class.'

Lorenzo Ebecilio might well be one such performer. But nobody, let alone Red Star Belgrade, would have known this, at least outside the clubs competing in Cyprus's Cyta Championship. Nobody, had it not been for the work of a senior member of one of these new analytics firms springing up to serve professional clubs at all levels.

Omar Chaudhuri was Head of Football Intelligence at 21st Club, a soccer consultancy based in London. Belgrade is a thousand miles from London, and Cyprus double that distance, but technology reinforces the notion of soccer as a global game. Chaudhuri had access to both the needs of Red Star Belgrade and the metrics of Lorenzo Ebecilio. He thought that the two could be a match and said as much to the authorities in Belgrade. Ebicilio was neither a figure on their radar, nor even one of whom they had heard. But they followed Chaudhuri's advice, took a look, and saw that they – or rather the soccer analyst – had discovered a gem; a player who would enhance a regular Champions League club for the fraction of the price they might have expected to pay for him.

'We're very much about trying to open the market up for clubs and discover undervalued talent,' said Choudhury.

Red Star had approached 21st Club with a profile of what they were after, and a list of potential players on a shortlist created by those players' agents. Hardly an objective group, we might conclude. The influence of agents is a constant concern in soccer transfers. These are people with a clear and vested interest in promoting their own player; their own income is dependent on their players. And their reputations. Quite why they have been allowed to become so influential in transfer proceedings is hard to determine. However, Red Star Belgrade had the foresight to use analytics to help them narrow down their shortlist. A perusal of the data by 21st Club demonstrated that not only was that shortlist lacking in identifying a player who could exactly match the requirements of the club, but that there was a better player out there, one who would cost a lot less money.

Ebecilio was duly signed and was soon helping to guide Red Star Belgrade to the group stages of the Champions League and making a mark against the likes of Liverpool and Paris St Germain. But

Choudhury is keen to stress that analytics are not (yet) the sole answer. Unsurprisingly, few scouts operate in the Cyprus league, and so other sources of information are needed. Analytics can find their way into worlds normally ignored by the traditional routes for scouting players. However, the data provided is just a part of the story. Choudhury makes it clear that a mixture of good data, good scouting and then the club stepping in to ensure that the player fulfils their requirements is the best way to secure a hidden treasure.

One of the founders of 21st Club is a former Prozone employee. Blake Wooster explains the rationale behind his business, and its name. He and his fellow founders started from the premise of imagining they were the bottom club of a league, the imaginary 21st place. They then sought to identify what they would need to give them an edge sufficient to compete, and survive, in their league.

This in turn led Wooster to identify that the route to marginal gains lay in identifying the inefficiencies in the way soccer operates. Although a soccer fan, he identified that it was not soccer professionals who would help to identify those inefficiencies. It would be analysts, software designers, management consultants and suchlike. People who could work with teams to help them identify their strategies, and then implement them. It takes little thinking to understand the common sense of this.

Managers and coaches are overwhelmingly ex pros. People whose own younger years were spent playing the game at every opportunity, committing to their sporting career rather than their educational ones. It is far too simplistic to identify professional sports players as somehow academically lacking, but equally there are few top sportsmen and women, in soccer especially, and in the men's game more so, who had the time to commit to their studies in the way their peers could manage. Such players do exist – the former Chelsea stalwart and current manager Frank Lampard is a notable example – but they are in a minority.

Therefore, it is completely understandable that a soccer coach has likely not gained the sorts of skills required for running a major organisation such as a soccer club. These are people who committed themselves to becoming the best soccer player they could be, then completed their coaching badges before working at getting a job and establishing a career in management. It is no surprise that they should now seek to benefit from the services of consultants from other fields.

PIRLO – Case Study of An Analytics Programme

Into this void stepped 21st Club. They called upon the Italian midfield maestro Pirlo to name their analytics engine. Standing for Predictive Intelligence Research and Learning Outcomes – I think we can agree that Pirlo rolls off the tongue more easily.

By 2018 Pirlo had gathered and processed data about no less than 150000 players. It employs machine learning algorithms, such as the ones used by major global players such as Amazon, to offer insights into players who would not normally feature on a club's radar.

Remember, the premise behind PIRLO is that clubs at the bottom of their particular pile need to identify ways in which they can close the gap on those above them in the soccer playing pyramid. Immediately a weakness in the use of analytics by clubs was identified by the company. Both in the media, and significantly in many clubs, in identifying possible transfer targets the focus tends to be on easily assimilated statistics – goals scored, assists, tackles, passing and so forth. These are all very well, but soccer players are humans, not machines. There are a variety of factors which will determine whether or not they can reproduce the statistics which are used in identifying them as a transfer target in the first place.

They factors are myriad – they include the players around them, changes to their roles in a team, the relative strength of opponents. Then there are changes to training regimes. Perhaps hardest to determine are the cultural and social impacts on a player when they change clubs, and especially if that transfer means going to a new country. Simply, a player who is not happy will not perform as well. This is true of any person in any walk of life. A common response to this fact goes along the lines of '$50000 per week should make anybody happy.' No doubt it helps, but any person with money knows that it is not the answer to everything. Particularly, happiness.

21st Club sought to break new ground. They felt they needed to specialise, and sought to gain a clear understanding of how players from the Dutch Eredivisie would cope in other leagues. It became apparent, very quickly, that on the one hand there were many unfished rivers of cheap talent around, and also that rich clubs were wasting a lot of money on players who would not justify their price tags. For example, score a goal in a world cup, and your transfer fee rises by 15%.

Innovative companies such as 21st Club are proving that just as technology can disrupt the priveliged castles enjoyed exclusively by industry giants, so it can do the same to the world of soccer.

Rich clubs…watch out.

Case Study – Replacing Star Players in High Performing Clubs

Another system that can be used involves assessing player possession motifs, or PPMs. These data driven assessments identify playing patterns of players, specifically the way they interact with their team mates with passing moves. PPMs can be grouped into similar playing patterns so that when a player moves, or loses form, they can be replaced by another who will operate in a similar way. Thus, when Lahm began to age at Bayern Munich, replacing him with Alba would have seen a similar playing style replicated. Conversely, when a player is purchased and asked to perform a different job at a club, there is a significant chance that the player will be less successful. Wise coaches change a player's style with caution.

But players do leave; they do get older and slow down. They do get injured. Arsenal and Manchester United dominated the Premier League during the late 1990s and early 2000s. The visionary leader Arsene Wenger identified that the Arsenal traditional business structure – with significant fan shares, and a proper board running the club, rather than a wealthy owner – meant that the club would need another source of income to compete at the top level. That meant increasing stadium capacity, something impossible in the club's Highbury home, surrounded as it was on all sides by housing.

And so the club invested in a new stadium; the 60000+ capacity at the magnificent Emirates Stadium is a joy to visit, but the cost meant that Arsenal lost their place at the head of the top table of English soccer, and had to take on a side seat, albeit, still at the top. Ironically, a very wealthy owner did take over the club – Stan Kroenke, controversial sports tycoon whose main interests seem to lie in other sports in the US. That was in 2011, and many fans point to this as the stage at which the club began a slow descent.

Nevertheless, by 2015/2016, two of the finest players in the world graced the green grass of the Emirates – Mesut Ozil and Alexis Sanchez. However, as Arsene Wenger's reign became under increasing threat it became clear that one, or perhaps both, would soon look to leave. It was Sanchez who eventually went (highly unsuccessfully, to Manchester United). Yet much of Arsenal's success in the early and mid-2010s was down to these two players; top four finishes were still securing Champions League football and the club was successful in cup competitions.

However, analysis demonstrated another player who was heavily significant in Sanchez's goalscoring – left back Nacho Monreal. Unfortunately, the player became injury prone. Analysis could inform the Arsenal board who might be purchased to replace these players without changing the team's structure or fast flowing, possession-based playing style. One of the replacements for Ozil identified by PPM – the passing and possession style of the player – and their goal scoring and chance creating style identified James Rodriguez, then of Real Madrid, with whom Arsenal were linked for a long time. In the end Ozil stayed, Wenger left as did Monreal. Without Sanchez in front of him, he was not quite the same player in his final season at Arsenal, although injuries could have been a factor in this.

Yet it is not just players who contribute to a team's success and style. Even more significant is the coach. During the club's dominance of the league, Manchester United's Alex Ferguson and Arsenal's Arsene Wenger were ever present. Both led for well over twenty years, and both effectively ran their clubs, handling all aspects linked directly to play. Their longevity was truly remarkable in the results driven modern game. Arsenal had a slight advantage in seeing the impact of a very long serving manager departing, as Manchester United imploded in the season's following Ferguson's retirement.

However, despite the analytics available, the Arsenal board appeared determined to abandon the twenty plus years of successful strategy. By using their in-house data team, they could reasonably have identified coaches who would build on Wenger's legacy, addressing weaknesses in the team while still allowing the players to keep with the style established. Given that money at the club has been much tighter in recent years, such a philosophy would seem sensible.

The best analytics to have been used here would have been a combination of team passing and possession motifs, known as TPMs, and team expected goals figures (TxGMs).

From this information, five potential managers would have emerged as likely successors. Big names would include Massimiliano Allegri and Antonio Conte. The forward-thinking approach of Juventus is highlighted here. When their coach, Conte, left ultimately for

Chelsea in 2015 the club replaced him with Allegri, who maintained success by basing team plays and tactics on similar strategies as Conte.

Unfortunately for the fans, Arsenal did not demonstrate the same level of forward thinking. Even if Conte and Allegri were outside of their price range, Lucien Favre at Borussia Monchengladbach and (more recently) Luciano Spaletti at AS Roma would have followed in Wenger's footsteps without needing a substantial change of shoe. Among the shortlisted candidates were the untried Mikel Arteta, who would eventually take over at Arsenal following the failed spell under Unai Emery, other former players including Thierry Henry and Patrick Vieira and indeed Allegri. Two international managers, each of whom would later see their value diminish, were short-listed, Jorge Sampaoli and Julien Lopetegui. The promising RB Leipzig coach, Ralph Rangnick completed the line-up.

Thus, in Allegri plus the former players (albeit two with no managerial experience at the time, the other, Vieira, with only limited experience) it was clear that the intention was to *consider* retaining the style Wenger established. Or, was this just a sop to fans?

Apparently, so the story goes, Emery was not on the original short list, but like the outsider in a horse race, started progressing on the rails, was called for interview and blew away the opposition.

But as those who back outsiders know, one victory does not always translate into long term success. Just like one goal in a world cup does not make you a 15% better player. Perhaps the appointment of Emery offers a pertinent lesson on the importance of considering analytics. It had been known for a while that defensively Arsenal were not as strong as they should be. Further, their key defender Laurent Koscielny was increasingly injury prone and clearly considering a return to France to end his career. The highly reliable Per Mertesacker had just retired, and Shodran Mustafi was unfortunately predisposed to the odd, crucial, error when exposed. At full back, the reliable Monreal was, as stated above, susceptible to injury and the powerful Hector Bellerin was excellent going forward but could be caught out positionally when defending. Petr Cech, the goalkeeper, had been perhaps the world's best in the past, but his career was coming to an end.

On top of that, the heart of the midfield, Aaron Ramsey, had decided to move on to a new role at Juventus. (This did not work out, illustrating the risk of taking a player successful at performing in one way, and expecting them to play in another). This was never the collection of players to take on a team strategy based around effective defense, especially away from home.

Analysis of the data would have demonstrated the sort of team Emery was likely to seek to create, and to prove that this particular group of players would not be able to deliver it. A problem exacerbated by years of the short passing, high risk 'Wenger way' and the lack of money to bring in replacements.

Elsewhere in this book we have challenged the tradition of soccer teams employing its own in coaching and player management roles. Rightly so, given that such an approach means change takes longer to occur. However, in this case study there is opposite evidence. The group that appointed Unai Emery to the post of head coach were businessmen, not soccer men. For once, their limitations in understanding the game was demonstrated.

THE CHALLENGE OF APPLYING ANALYTICS IN SOCCER

Is soccer less suited to analytics than other sports?

'The first ninety minutes are the most important.' England Manager
Bobby Robson

'Have you ever seen a statistic score a goal?' Ha. The argument won. It is the very complexity of soccer that makes the development of effective analytics so much of a challenge and, therefore, such a lucrative field of those operating within it. The difficulty of effective analysis of the various components that mix to make up the beautiful game are further challenged by the antithesis that lays deeply entrenched in its history. 'Soccer is a traditional game. A working-class past time founded in the parks of the industrial heartlands of England and developed on the streets of industrial cities in Europe and the beaches of Brazil. It is a tough game, where men are men and women are…' The argument soon falls down. Modern soccer is all inclusive, the most global team sport on the planet. In fact, it was never just a sport for the factory worker or miner. Consider the early days. The oldest competition in the world is the English FA Cup. For its first twelve finals the Wanderers – made up of players from English Public Schools and named because they were a nomadic team, playing at different stadiums, appeared and won five times. The Royal Engineers, consisting of officers of the Regiment, won once and were runners up on three occasions. Old Etonians, ex pupils of the famous Public School, appeared in four finals, winning once. This record was matched by that hotbed of diversity and educational opportunity for the working class, the Victorian Oxford University. Soccer might have been played by the working class at its outset, but it was never exclusively for this group.

We can therefore conclude that those who believe the use of analytics is somehow a betrayal of its roots rather than an enhancement of its future are wrong. That is not to say that the road to the ultimate stadium is anything but a long and very windy one. Take the case of a successful Engineering professor, Luis Amaral. The expert in using analytics to design complex social and structural networks in fields outside of sport turned his attention to soccer because it is his favourite entertainment. Amaral, along with his students, developed a complex system of coding techniques and metrics to create an AFR, or average footballer rating, for each player performing at a high level over the globe. The rating reflected their influence on matches. From this, he is able to identify the world's best players, objectively. During his study in the lead up to the 2018 world cup, his algorithm identified the best three players as Lionel Messi, Neymar Jr. and Cristiano Ronaldo.

Quite reasonably cynics might state that they could identify those superstars as the best without reference to complex analytics, and also that it is not only strikers who determine games. Common sense dictates that a team with a strong forward line but weak defense will win little. But, of course, that is common sense. One of the most oxymoronic of terms in the English language. It might be sense, or it might not, but it certainly is not common. Everybody's common sense is unique to them and is determined by a combination of numerous influences. Few of those influences being, of course, objective.

The very best players under Amaral's model, which could prove a huge benefit to coaches seeking to purchase players to strengthen already strong teams, have an AFR of over 70. The top of this elite maintain that AFR over a number of seasons.

What makes Amaral's analytics so interesting is that his system is designed for the flow sports, such as hockey, basketball or rugby. Tackling set piece sports such as American Football, cricket and so forth, is much easier since the sports divide much more neatly into set pieces and individual contests. Amaral's system takes the AFR of players in a team and produces a complex model of interaction in which both the players and the connections they have with team mates is objectively produced. What comes out looks like the sort of web a spider on speed might create. The thicker and more numerous the lines connecting the 'nodes' (the players) the stronger the interaction of the team, and therefore, in all likelihood, the more effective the team. But added to this each player or node varies in size and colour; large and dark indicating a more effective player than those represented by lighter, or smaller, nodes.

Amaral checked his system on the 2008 Euro championships, won by Spain and in which Xavi was named best player. His analytics indicated that Spain were the best team, and the star performer would be, statistically, Xavi. Encouraging.

In May 2018 he produced a model indicating his prediction of who would emerge as the best player in the upcoming world cup in each outfield position.

His conclusions demonstrated that there remains a long way to go before analytics can be completely relied upon! Qualitative analytics, PPMs and AFR might offer a more complete help to soccer coaches than pure statistical data, but analytics for flow sports is still in its infancy.

His predicted team was:

Defense:

Full backs - Alves and Marcelo of Brazil. Brazil made the quarter finals before being knocked out by Belgium.

Central defense - Ramos of Spain (knocked out in the last sixteen) and the German Hummels. Germany, notoriously, did not even get out of the group stages.

Midfield:

Here Amaral predicted Messi, Casemiro and De Bruyne of Belgium. De Bruyne certainly did have a fine world cup, being named as one of FIFA's finalists for the title of best player. Argentina, though, struggled through the group stages and were eliminated in the last sixteen by the eventual winners, France.

Attack:

Neymar from Brazil, Poland's Lewandowski (Poland failed to clear the group stages) and Ronaldo of Portugal, who were also knocked out in the last sixteen.

So, no mention of the break through young player, France's Kylian Mbappe; no prediction that Harry Kane of England would win the Golden Boot by a distance. No recognition of Antoine Griezmann, Romelu Lukaku, Eden Hazard or the midfield maestro Luka Modric?

Amaral failed to pick a player from either of the two nations who made the final, and only one player from the top four teams. Analytics are going in the right direction. But, as Amaral himself admits, they can be a great aid to a coach, but are not a magic answer to soccer's conundrums. At least, not yet. The assistance analytics offer to basketball is still way ahead of what it can offer to soccer.

It still remains simpler to find effective analytics for 'set piece' sports, or individual ones. Consider how easy it is to assess the strength of a tennis opponent compared to a soccer team, and therefore how much easier it is to develop a strategy to counter that tennis playing opponent. (Notwithstanding, as much as player one can develop a strategy to negate player two's driven top spin backhand – keep the ball on his or her forehand, being a starting point – so player two will be working hard on negating player one's negation!)

In golf, for example, it is relatively easy to work out which club to use depending on the lie of the ball, the distance to the tee, the prevailing weather conditions and the obstructions which might cause an issue. This is not to oversimplify golf; there is still pressure on the golfer making his or her shot; still tactical decisions to make as to whether to take risks or play safe. Still, when it comes to data, with modern technology, such information is readily available in the higher echelons of the game.

But the playing field is changing in soccer and the effectiveness of analytics is evening up.

But the playing field is changing. And quickly. Who would consider when Petr Cech looked at his list of likely penalties he would face that within five years systems would be available to measure and assess patterns of play, not just the statistical aspects of performance. As technology improves – both the data gathering technology and the software and algorithms used to assess it – more qualitative metrics are becoming available to coaches. This allows them to measure not only the technical elements of a particular soccer skill, but also its impact on the game.

As this qualitative analytical information becomes ever more accurate and useful, soccer will continue to evolve at pace. Whether that will place the world's richest clubs at an even greater advantage, or alternatively level the playing field back to the games earlier days remains to be seen. The extent to which analytics will cascade down to grass roots football too is hard to predict. Currently, it seems highly unlikely that the sort of flow analytics professional clubs are increasingly using will ever be accessible to a youth team coach. But, thirty years ago, who would envisage watching a soccer match from the other side of the world on your telephone?

SOCCER'S GREAT DEBATE: MESSI OR RONALDO?

How to use data analysis to break down the opposition.

Another piece of analysis which is important is one over which the coach has no control, but which is nevertheless significant in breaking down an opposition. That is the role of home advantage. There lies a conundrum. It definitely exists. On average, teams playing at home win almost half of the time and lose only thirty per cent of the time. One in four games are drawn. During home matches a typical team will create 7.6% more effective possession moves, and their expected goals ratio is higher by nearly a third compared to playing away. The Spanish club Sevilla, under the guidance of coach Unai Emery, demonstrated an enormous difference between home and away tactics. At home, over the three consecutive seasons when they were victorious in the Europa League, they consistently created around 50% more passing and possession moves than when they were playing away.

In a way, this might explain their success in the European competition, especially when the two-legged knock out stages came into force. Hard to beat away from home, as they packed in behind the ball, they could then take more risks in their home legs with their ebullient passing game. In fact, analysis suggests that over those seasons Sevilla's home performances reflected those of the best teams on the continent, whilst if they reproduced their away form at home as well, they would find themselves fighting relegation season on season.

Interestingly, Emery went on to manage Paris St Germain with good domestic success, but in the French Ligue 1 there is little competition for the mega-wealth of that club but gained little joy in Europe. He then moved to Arsenal, where the system enjoyed with Sevilla was replicated to a degree. But this time, relatively unsuccessfully. Arsenal were hard to beat at home, but their away form was of relegation standard. In his one full season at the North London club, he again repeated his success with the Europa League, taking the team to the final. Also like Sevilla, they did not come close to challenging for the league title, however.

The new coach was largely unpopular with fans at Arsenal. Stories leaked out. Emery was not respected by the players. Especially, a group of younger, up and coming ones. He was mocked for his heavy accent and poor English. 'Goo ebening,' they would mock, behind a smile, echoing the mis-pronounced phrase of which he was fond.

Other stories made their way onto social media, and into the back pages of the press. Yes, Emery was generally liked – he was enthusiastic and affable. But players did not understand his tactics. They were unclear what was required of them. Most leading clubs these days have a changing room with many native languages. It is to his credit that he tried to communicate in English. But whilst his effort might get a 'Tried hard' sticker in the end of term assembly, his progress in the language was D- at best. Emery is also an excitable character, and when the adrenalin flows through his veins, his English deteriorates further.

There are two images which stick in the mind in particular. Both came in the final games of his Arsenal career. Each occurred in the sometimes hostile atmosphere of the club's Ashburton Grove home. In the first, the opponents are Crystal Palace, a team the home side should win. The captain is Granit Xhaka, a Swiss international and fine player, but one who has acquired the ire of some sections of the crowd. He is becoming a scapegoat for the team's failings. Emery substitutes him early in the second half. There is booing; not for the decision but aimed at the captain. What followed caused an enormous fuss on social media and in the press; in fact, it was much less unpleasant than reports suggest. Nevertheless, Xhaka reacts to the boos, and lip readers looking at posted images later see him swearing. In the stadium, he merely looks angered at being substituted.

Emery seems unsure how to react, is visibly upset, and loses the plot. As Arsenal struggle, he removes firstly the right sided centre back of three. Then the right full back. A back five has turned into a back three – fair enough, given the game is not going Arsenal's way, but somehow there is a failure to communicate who is to fill the right side defense position. Palace cannot believe their luck. They rush into the open spaces now on their left, and cause mayhem.

In the other example, which turns out to be Emery's final home match, he can be seen gesticulating wildly – manically even – from his technical area. He paces like a trapped bear who can smell honey but cannot reach it. Up and down he moves, screaming instructions and pointing to positions. But any remaining vestiges of faith in him are gone. The players ignore the instructions he is trying to give. It is a sad end to a manager's dream.

The point is illustrated clearly that whatever the tactics, if there is a failure to communicate, teams become less effective. Most probably because those complex possession and passing moves which are central to success break down.

But also, there is the general observation that in establishing how opponents are likely to set up coaches must consider whether they are at their home, or travelling. It makes a difference.

A particular tool a coach can use to assess an opponent's playing style is to look at the player possession motifs of their opponents. Such information can be collected by their own in-house analytics teams or purchased from the commercial companies operating ever more widely. The nature of how a team plays is built around its passing strategy.

Which player tends to come and collect the ball off the back four? Where do they tend to pass? Does the team look to build on one side of the pitch and switch play? How do they operate in transition, the most dangerous time for the defending team who have just lost the ball?

Who supplies passes into the box? The list is endless and player possession motifs will help to define, through the complex networks they produce, which players collect the ball and what they do with it when they have it.

Statistical evidence of the quantitive variety can be used to predict opponent's play from set pieces, both offensive and defensive. Typical team formations can be assessed from empirical evidence, and plays developed to counter this. As we saw at the outset of the chapter, whether the team is home or away is likely to affect their playing style.

A good starting point when looking at using data to help break down the opposition's game is to negate their main goal threat.

We can take a very available example to illustrate this, comparing the two best players in the world for the past decade, Lionel Messi and Cristiano Ronaldo. What analytics will tell us is that Messi must be stopped at source, before he can create flowing moves and chances for himself and others. Ronaldo, while still a great threat in all respects, offers less threat from deep, or earlier in a move. Messi demonstrates himself as a far more complete attacking player; he both becomes heavily involved in the build up to his goal scoring chances, but also provides many assists, or involvement in moves that lead to goals for others.

Barcelona noted this and purchased the Uruguayan Luis Suarez to benefit from Messi's creativity. Thus, a team looking to stop Messi must halt his progress much earlier in a move, before he can develop it into a goal scoring opportunity. Awareness of this has led to the oft made claim that Messi can go quiet for long periods, before bursting into life with a goal or assist. Where he does dominate for long periods, it is likely that the opposing coach has failed to instil into his team the importance of stopping Messi from early on in a move.

Although, of course, such an ambition is much easier planned than achieved!

By contrast, Ronaldo scores very different types of goals to his arch competitor for the title of 'World's Best Player'. Earlier in his career, especially at Real Madrid (he more often played wide when at Manchester United), his team's game plan seemed to involve simply getting the ball to him quickly, and then let him use his pace, strength, shooting power and heading ability to secure an attempt at goal. This may well have been an influence on Real's willingness to break all transfer records in purchasing Gareth Bale, a very direct player who could play through the middle, like Ronaldo, or wide, like Ronaldo. Thus, the goal threat would be doubled. Equally, Bale's crossing ability could create more chances for Ronaldo to score.

Over a couple of seasons, opponents got used to this approach, and understood that by reducing the supply to Ronaldo, his impact would be (to some extent) neutralised. Later in his Real Madrid career, the coaching philosophy changed to a less direct approach, with players seeking to build up more slowly before releasing the key pass. Still, though, Ronaldo's goal scoring tended to feature him only in the end stage of the move.

On more mortal levels, a coach can set up his team to deal with the most significant goal threat. Does it involve stopping a player early in a move? Is it about cutting the supply chain? Does a defender shift him on to his weaker foot? It is the data, quantitative (e.g., percentage of goals scored with shots inside the area with the stronger foot) and qualitative (an illustration here could be the movement and interaction of players that lead to his goal scoring chances) that will inform this decision. So, for example, a team such as Leicester during their championship winning season could be negated by pressurising their defense to reduce the accuracy of the long balls they played in behind their opponents' defence for the likes of Jamie Vardy and Riyad Mahrez from turning their defenders, and forcing them to chase back. The explosive speed of Vardy and Mahrez meant that once they did get in behind, the chances of a goal scoring opportunity were massively increased.

If the defense line were pressured, the accuracy of their long passing would be compromised meaning that Vardy and co would be less effective in their opponents' half.

To return to the soon to end Messi v Ronaldo debate over who is the better player, analytics such as their passing and possession profiles really stop the argument. Messi scores more regularly (at the time of writing). One goal every one and a quarter games, compared to just under one in every one and a third games for the Juventus striker.

Those figures are for all games including internationals. At club level Messi provides 25% more assists, in fewer games. But that only tells a little of the story. What quantitative data does not tell is the impact of player in the build-up. An assist is important, but it is only one small part of a goal. Messi's involvement – because he plays naturally a little deeper of the two – is greater, according to what qualitative analysis is available.

Messi does not have it all his own way, though. Interestingly, on the biggest club stage, Europe, Ronaldo more or less matches his goal per game and assist stats for all club football. Messi, though slips a little when it comes to assist rates from around one in three to one in four in Europe. His goal scoring remains around the same. Perhaps the generally higher standard of club operating in the Champions League are better at cutting Messi out before he can make the killer pass.

When it comes to La Classico – matches between the Spanish giants Real Madrid and Barcelona – Messi wins hands down. That, though, might reflect Barca's better record in La Liga. Messi scores slightly more regularly and wins almost twice the number of times. But again, it is in all round performance that the Argentinian dominates. In thirty-eight games, he has made 14 assists and created 68 chances. Ronaldo, by comparison, has just one assist and 15 chances created in his thirty games.

Nevertheless, while Ronaldo could well be the best finisher in the world (he has thirty three more goals than Messi in total – the Argentinian only just breaking the 700 mark – come on Lionel, put your shooting boots on!), in terms of all-round performance Messi is ahead. That the diminutive Argentinian also scores a comparable number of goals to Ronaldo, whilst still contributing a significant number of assists supports the view that he is the better player. His involvement in the creation of goal scoring opportunities surely settles the argument. Messi is the king, at least in terms of what he contributes to his team. Anybody disagree?

ANALYTICS, SET PIECES AND SET PLAYS

How analytics can be used to improve a team's strategy in dead ball situations

'This (throw ins) is a phase of play where the vast majority of teams produce nothing. Stoke produced a shot and a half a game just from throw ins during the Rory Delap years. If you are able to build and execute a long-throw program, it's the equivalent of making free goals out of thin air.' – Ted Knutson, analytics consultant on Tony Pulis and his long throw tactics.

We've already seen that the biggest red herring in soccer is the award of a corner. Statistically, according to the Outside of the boot website, a corner equates to 0.022 of a goal. That is not much of a deal when the corner is most likely to end up with the loss of possession. 0.022 of a goal equates, for an average team in a league playing about 40 matches a season to about four goals through the season, to less than one goal in sixteen corners, on average.

Real Salt Lake are a forward-looking team in the USA's MLS. They are relatively successful, having won the play offs on one occasion, and achieved a number of high league finishes. RSL is a club without the resources of some of their opponents, but one which has invested heavily in using analytics to close the money gap with bigger opponents.

They are one of a number of sides who made the tactical decision to commit two players to the taking of corners in order to improve the chances of scoring. Having two players available might seem illogical. The crowd want the ball swung into the box, and that takes only one corner taker. However, the second player doubles the options, since a short corner is now a possibility. This means that the defense need to commit two players to stopping the short corner, or at least forcing a cross from a still disadvantageous position.

Committing one is insufficient, since most teams in a 2 v 1 overload at a corner will be able to generate the space for a cross from a dangerous position – close in and from a good angle. Clearly, with only one player ready to take the corner, no defenders need to be pulled out of their position defending the goal since the only option is a cross in. Nothing short can be played.

The higher the number of players in a box the less likelihood there is of a goal, since attackers not only have to get to the ball first, but they must do so in a way that both allows a proper contact on the ball, and for it to have a clear route to goal. Overwhelmingly the number of free kicks in the penalty box from a corner favors the defense. After all, a free kick to an attacker is a penalty, and a very high chance of a goal. A referee has a much higher set of standards to reach to award such a game changing decision. A free kick to the defense merely restarts the game. The more players in the box, the higher the likelihood of an infringement occurring.

So, having two players out from the corner reduces the number of players in the box by at least three. The 'spare' attacker, and the two defenders pulled out to prevent a dangerous short corner.

But there is more that data analysis has demonstrated to make corners more effective. The sartorially elegant Italian former player and now coach Roberto Mancini won the Premier League in charge of the money flushed Manchester City. Instinctively, Mancini believed – along with many old pros – the out-swinging corner was the most dangerous. An inswinger is often cut off by the defender positioned outside the near post and is much more likely to be taken by the goalkeeper. Analysts, though, were able to present the data that demonstrated this is wrong. In the 2011-2012 season in which Mancini's team were crowned champions, the coach ordered a far higher percentage of corners to be inswingers. City scored an astonishing fifteen goals from this set piece during that season, and those goals proved significant in delivering the championship to them in what was a very tight final table.

Pure data analytics has demonstrated the most effective times for substitutions, and this has significantly changed game play. Where a team is losing, Dr Bret Myers, a former player and a professional working with analytics, has demonstrated that a losing team stand a better chance of getting back into a game if they apply the following rules: first substitution no later than the 58th minute, second before the 73rd minute and the final substitution must be made prior to the 79th minute. Following these statistical guidelines approximately doubles the chance of scoring at least one goal – up to 36% of the time compared to 18.5% of the time where coaches adopt a different strategy.

This data may well be linked to the current trend of early substitutions. Many coaches now make one or two (sometimes even three) changes at half time if their team's performance has not matched their game plan.

But what is emerging in this chapter, as we look at the impact of analytics on set pieces, is that much more information exists than is the case with the more fluid elements of soccer. Probably, that is inevitable. Moneyball focussed on baseball, which, like most bat and ball games, constantly breaks itself into set pieces. It can be of no surprise that analytics' influence on soccer begins in the same departments.

The former German striker Jurgen Klinsmann turned to management when his playing days were over and went on to coach Germany in a World Cup. A personal friend of Billy Beane, the Moneyball man, Klinsmann is much enamoured with the use of analytics in gaining an advantage in soccer. The coach consulted a data firm based in Cologne in an early example of seeking to use analytics to help influence matches, rather than simply to maintain an eye on player fitness and form. It worked well enough, Germany ending up in third place, albeit in a tournament on home soil. Most famously, in the quarter final against Argentina, the German keeper had written a list of notes on the opposing penalty takers should the game run to a shoot out. It did, and Jens Lehmann produced the list from inside his sock to consult before each penalty. It worked. Argentina scored only twice, and Germany staggered through to the semi-final.

No doubt the curly haired German keeper would have employed the same tactics there. With the full ninety played, and 29 of the thirty minutes of extra time completed, the teams were goalless, and a penalty shoot out beckoned. Then the eventual winners scored twice in the final minute to win through to the final, where they defeated France, again on penalties.

But that tournament did, in many ways, secure the future of analytics in the game. Eight games were played from the quarter finals onwards (quarters, semis, final and third place play off). Three of those were decided in a shoot out. Tactics were becoming so good that weaker teams were able to negate stronger ones, and something new was needed to break the stranglehold. In his small way, Jurgen Klinsmann was at the forefront of introducing that, along with the likes of Sam Allardyce at Bolton, and Arsene Wenger at Monaco and Arsenal.

Nowadays, though, as useful as the sort of pure, quantitative data is for preparing for set pieces – both offensive and defensive – it is being surpassed by the growth of qualitive analytics since they can demonstrate the value of strategy and technique in the context of the entire game.

Still, we can see how analytics have transformed the set piece elements of the game. Take free kicks, for example. It was not many years ago that any such set piece in the attacking half – or even close to the half way line – would be launched into the penalty box. Nowadays, such a tactic is very rare. Certainly, free kicks in shooting range will still usually result in a shot on goal, and in a wide position close to the box in a cross, but deeper free kicks will most often result in players using the award to restart their passing moves.

The unintended effect of this is that defenses can commit 'tactical' fouls – ones sufficient to break up an attack and give time for a defense to re-organise while the attacking side reset the ball and pass; referees are becoming wiser to this, and such fouls are increasingly punished with a yellow card.

However, it would be interesting to have access to the data on the award of these yellow cards – most fans will claim that the officials' interpretation of necessary punishment lacks consistency.

So, we can see how analytics have led to a change in strategic defensive tactics. Since analytics have demonstrated that launching a long ball into the box is not a constructive strategy, it is better for a team to keep possession. Sweeping moves on transition have been demonstrated as a very effective attacking technique. This can be stopped by a tactical foul, allowing defenses to get themselves reorganised. Referees are beginning to become stricter with such tactical fouls. There will come a point where teams commit less of them, because the risk of collecting yellow, and then red, cards becomes too great.

We can expect to see the analytics of this defensive strategy demonstrating that a new approach is needed to deal with breakaways before too long. At the moment, they show that conceding a free kick outside of shooting range is an infringement worth giving away.

We will conclude the chapter with two points. Firstly, common sense dictates that the evidence of quantitative analytics at set pieces states the obvious. The truth is very different; inswinging corners, zonal marking, use of the long throw, timings of substitutes, quick free kicks, keeping possession, plotting the likely trajectory of a penalty…all of these and more have been modified based on the evidence of analytics. Metrics really do change the game.

And finally, is there any more farcical sight in soccer than the latest trend in a defensive wall at a free kick? Data has clearly indicated that the shot driven below a jumping wall can be a threat. Unfortunately, the response of many teams is to leave a player prostrate and full length on the floor, arms hidden, in the hope that such a low drive will strike them, rather than the back of the net. A strategy that takes going to ground to whole new depths! Literally.

HOW DATA IS COLLECTED

We have mentioned already that Opta's collection of stats from the late 1990s was pretty blunt in its execution. Match records and historical statistics are all very well for the armchair analyst, or the keen child who wants to learn everything there is to know about their favourite team or player, but they tell us little about the game.

A clue that this data is not particularly useful for coaches is evident because it is so widely available. No, what coaches need are two sets of quite specific data. Firstly, they need data on individuals, to help them determine fitness, form, effectiveness during a game and to help keep them injury free. Secondly, they require complex data, not just statistics. Data which demonstrates how plays – tackles, passes, dribbles, shots and so forth – influence games. Therefore, the pure data needs to be combined with different layers of information such as where they occur on the pitch, the location of team mates and opposition at the time, the stage and state of the game at the time.

This information is the province of the large data providing organisations, the Optas, Prozones and such like. Their services are intensely expensive, and highly secretive. A fan is more likely to get an invite to their superstar soccer player's birthday party than to get an insight as to how their club's anonymous data analytics team use the information they gather.

There is, of course, a sad lesson here. High level analytics is, at present at least, a very exclusive shrine. Amateur coaches and youth team managers simply won't be able to afford access to such data. Perhaps that is a good thing. The data is about improving chances to win. Perhaps that is the realm of the professional game, and at amateur and youth level the purpose of soccer is to engineer team spirit, cooperation, social skills, physical and mental health. And most of all, fun. Winning is an unnecessary distraction from these key aims. Or, at least, the sort of obsession with winning which drives the professional game. Does a twelve-year-old player really need to know that they use up too much energy chasing lost causes, or pass to a friend more often than to a better placed team mate? Not really.

Still, where a coach really wants to get their hands on the sort of metrics which, in the simplest, most basic form, reflect what is going on at professional levels, then the growth of the analytics industry means that there are more companies operating, a lot of them smaller, independent services. Market forces mean that prices will be driven down over time.

At the professional level, we might divide modern analytics into three groups.

- The data that is gathered by clubs and the data companies that they employ.
- Analysis completed using data in the public domain (perhaps an indicator that amateur coaches could use to help them determine tactics and strategy)
- Finally, where commercial data is analysed independently.

It is worth noting that many of the bigger clubs nowadays have their own in-house data analytics arm. In 2013, for example, Arsenal purchased a US based analytics company called StatDNA. The purchase was hidden by the club's then chief executive, Ivan Gazidis. 'The company is an expert in the field of sports data performance analysis,' he told the club's annual general meeting, when pushed to explain the £2 million plus outlay. 'A rapidly developing area and one that I, and others, believe will be critical to Arsenal's competitive position,' he claimed. They are not alone, nor are they in employing a team of no less than eight analysts in their backroom team, there to interpret the data fed into them. It is interesting to note that the club employs more analysts than first team coaching staff.

They are not alone.

These days, at the highest level of the game, clubs are heavily involved with collecting data. Ten or more digital cameras will track every player in the team. Astonishingly, no less than ten data points are collected every second for every player involved in the game. That equates to an eye boggling 1.4 million data points for every match. The raw data is then interpreted by an analytics firm such as Prozone, or by the clubs' own analytics in house services. Codes are applied to the raw information, and that information is translated to identify everything the player does, both in contact with the ball and off the ball. Thus, the coach, manager and his team can have an accurate and inciteful breakdown of what takes place in the game.

When this is added to the use of heart monitors, GPS trackers and acceleration trackers mentioned earlier we can see that the modern professional footballer is exposed to a huge range of technology. Added to this, regular medical testing will help to confirm optimum muscle development, stamina and endurance. Although currently obtaining the data might be less high tech, players are also subject to dietary monitoring, sleep monitoring and rest. Mental health is increasingly understood both in terms of the players' wellbeing, but also in their performance.

A player who is mentally below peak condition will be unlikely to perform as well as one who is strong in this respect. Mental strengthening through the use of sports psychologists is nowadays a regular part of a player's daily routine.

CAN ANALYTICS CAN HELP PREDICT TRENDS?

The answer to the above chapter title question is a resounding 'Yes'. Even if early stats collection was utilitarian in nature (no doubt, in ten years, whoever is writing the latest version of this book will make the same observation about the collection of analytics in the 2010s.) But quite quickly, they enabled an analysis of trends in the game. In fact, the data not only predicted those trends, but it was able to do so because it was setting them. We have the evidence that set piece play led to the scoring of more goals. Charles Clarke, the English technical coaching director identified that in the France 98 World Cup most goals were scored after just a short number of passes. Each of these data conclusions led to the development of the long ball game.

If that tactic in soccer had its groundings in the poor quality of pitches – it is hard to dribble like a Messi if playing on a cow field – now its development was based on statistical data. There was an interesting, if logical, outcome to this trend; tall strikers began to attract a transfer premium. If teams were beginning to base their play around a long ball game, with the strategy of winning free kicks, then players who could hold the ball up, and win duels in the box, became highly prized. Too highly prized, meaning that bargains could be found by investing in smaller, more skilful and mobile strikers. The big boy bubble burst, and the trend started for these diminutive strikers who could dribble, pass and run.

Such changes in the game were tracked by the data, and that very data began to show a shift from set piece dominant tactics to more mobile and fluid attacking. The sort of player who could deliver a dead ball with unerring accuracy, or pull in a cross from the wing, began to diminish. Still important, yes, but no longer crucial to a team's strategy. One is left wondering whether David Beckham, for example, would have become such a global name had he been playing today, where his key skills of hitting a dead ball and passing over great distances would still be useful, but not the basis for his team's game management.

It was around 2003, when Beckham was at his height, that the limitations of the kind of stats which provided huge benefit for 'set piece' sports, such as basketball, began to be exposed. It seems astonishing that even today, nearly twenty years on, TV coverage focusses so much on stats such as shots on target, or distances run by players. That data is almost irrelevant within the context of a game. A side might have twenty shots at goal, but if three quarters of them are from distance, the chances are they will not score. However, an opponent who creates five scoring opportunities, five shots at goal, but all from strong positions, is far more likely to win the game. Atletico Madrid, under the tutelage of the pragmatic Diego Simeone, illustrates this to perfection. When Leicester City won their title, they generally enjoyed a significant minority of possession but made excellent use of it when they had it, turning it into a high percentage of goal scoring opportunities.

As fans of the game, but perhaps not experts, we can be hoodwinked into placing too much emphasis on this data. The big companies, with their golden money tree in sight, but out of reach, set about redesigning the way analytics could be used.

And if stats were to be redesigned, then the way they influence the game would be as well. A very good example can be found in watching the post-match analysis of games by ex-pro, pundit, experts (the terms, to be fair, to be used with diminishing levels of certainty). Especially when looking at defense formations. How often with the grizzled, broken nosed former centre half break down a goal conceded and notify their audience that the defenders 'are not close enough to each other'?

But analytics has demonstrated truth in this gut instinct and experience. In fact, the optimum distance for defenders to be apart is eight metres. But now everybody knows that, because the stats do not lie (usually), and so coaches seek new ways of attack into to disrupt this defensive organisation. The high press could be said to be a tactic born out of a direct response of the learning imbued by analytics.

If a team are playing out from the back, which they must do if they wish to be sure of keeping possession – itself a usual, but not inevitable, indicator of increased likelihood of winning – they must find space. Usually this will manifest itself by one or both full back pushing on, leaving a much bigger than eight metre gap from their colleagues in the back four or five. Thus, if a team makes a successful high press, they will win the ball and be faced with a defense who are not eight metres apart and in perfect formation. In winning the ball, the high pressing team will have a few moments to exploit they space they have before the defense can recover its organisation. At the highest levels, a few moments are all that is needed to score.

We can see also how analytics can be used to set up against an individual in an opposing side. Take a dribbler like Lionel Messi. By studying footage, it is now known that the best way of stopping a Messi run is to use two defenders, one directly in front of the fleet footed Argentinian, the other approximately a metre behind. It might reasonably be said, though, that this is hardly earth shattering. In the days when wingers were wingers and shorts were longs, dribbling seemed to play a much larger role in the game than it does today. The best way to stop a dribbler was to double up, ie one player shepherds, and a team mate is there to sweep up when the dribbler goes past.

There must be a moment when the attacking player knocks the ball a little further on in order to take it past the first defender. This is when the second defender moves in.

The other problem with this undoubtedly correct method of stopping players like Messi is that it often doesn't work. If it did, then we would have no Messis or Di Marias or Zahas in the game, and it would be a lesser game for that.

THE NEW BATTLE – TRADITIONALISTS V ANALYSTS

We started this book by considering the role of the ex-pro, particularly when they appear on TV in a role of a pundit, and the negativity they sometimes have with regards to modern developments in the game. This is often delivered with more than a touch of self-deluded irony. The tough talking centre half, the take no prisoners midfield 'enforcer' will castigate lack of decision making, lack of bottle, lack of technique, lack of mettle of the modern day player, hark back to the days when training consisted of twice round the local park and a few bruised ankles from the five a side and do so whilst using the latest video analysis technology.

This brings us back to luck – the antithesis of analytics. It is hard to argue that luck does not play some role in all sport, and therefore soccer as well, but not as much as is frequently claimed. Let us take a look at golf for a moment, one of those sports where the variable of what an opponent does has little impact on one's own performance. Maybe, if on a blustery day, the wind strikes up just at the moment our drive from the tee is heading down the middle of the fairway, and the ball is suddenly blown into the rough. Maybe. Then again, analysts would identify that the player would know it was a blustery day, and therefore the best players would change the trajectory of their drive, sacrificing a little distance for the benefit of a flat shot which would be less impacted on by the wind.

Certainly, when Lee Trevino looked certain to have lost the 1972 British Open after finding himself in the rough just off the green, luck played no part. Despite famous claims to the opposite. On that occasion, Tony Jacklin – a very successful player of those flared trousered days who never quite managed to fulfil his potential in a major – was tied for the lead with Trevino on the penultimate hole of the championship. He was well set to down his putt while Trevino looked to be in the position where a chip and two putts would be the best he could hope for.

Trevino chipped…straight into the hole. Luck? Not at all. Where was Trevino aiming? The hole. How many hours had he spent working on shots such as this? Where was the most likely single spot the ball would end up? In the hole. Then, golf fans will know, Jacklin not only missed his putt, but the follow up as well. Bad luck? Or pressure?

Another golfer, the great South African Gary Player, once said: 'The harder I work, the luckier I get.' The tennis genius Bjorn Borg was another blessed with luck. Watch recordings of his matches and note the number of times his shots striker the top of the net, trickle over and fall to the other side before dribbling to a point winning halt.

Clearly, Borg was merely a good player who got the rub of the green. Again. And again. And again! Not that the Swede, or his trainers, knew that if he hit the ball with huge force and immense top spin with the wooden headed rackets of yesteryear, aiming flat and low to give his opponent the least possible chance to make a return, he would win more points. That in doing so, if his shot was a fraction out, a little too low, the probability was the power and top spin of his drive would lift the ball up and over as it made contact with the net.

Or we could look at snooker. Surely, the only sport in the world played in two thirds of a three-piece suit, complete with bow tie. One of the finest proponents of the game in the 1980s and 90s was the Londoner Jimmy White. The Whirlwind, as he was known. (Meteorological nicknames were popular back then. If one survived the Whirlwind, the Hurricane was usually there in the next round, Irishman Alex Hurricane Higgins, that is.) White was an outstanding player, known for his speedy break building and cockney wit. He reached six world finals…and lost them all. The reason? Not, as his many fans claim, bad luck. The rub of the green (baize) going against him. Of all sports, snooker (along with billiards and pool) really are luck free. Every factor can be controlled. The balls will behave exactly as physics dictates. Potting is mathematical in its calculation of angles. When a wayward red breaks in front of the black ball the player was hoping to pot that is not bad luck, but it relates to how the previous shot was hit.

Jimmy White lost six finals not because he was unlucky but on the day (or days, being snooker) his various opponents were better. That on four occasions this was the best player in the world at the time, Stephen Hendry, and on one other Steve Davis, then just about unbeatable puts the record into context. In 1991, he also lost to the little-known Jon Parrot. Certainly, in world history White is a better player, but in 1991 Parrot has his annus mirablis, and hit heights he would never achieve again.

There is another factor which may have contributed to White's relative failure. Psychological factor. The pressure of playing a final is impossible to calculate. Especially in a sport like snooker where, once an opponent is at the table, a player has absolutely no ability whatsoever to influence the game.

It is hard to ever mention snooker without a brief reference to the ultra-talented Canadian Bill Wierbeneck. The rotund but explosive player was always entertaining, but never quite achieved the heights his talent suggested. That he could down as much as eight pints of lager – for medicinal reasons, of course – may have had more of an effect on his eventual downfall than luck. Or talent, for that matter.

The point we are making here is that luck really does play the smallest of parts in the outcome of sports matches. Soccer included. What counts towards results in soccer are the physical fitness and mental strength of players; the skill and technique of the participants. The tactics employed by coaches, and the ability of players to respond collectively to the tactics of opponents. Certainly, the decision making of the referee is a variable harder to control, because most decisions by officials in soccer are subjective. The use of VAR (the video assistant referee) attempts to soften the subjectivity of such decisions, but this is still in its infancy as a tool.

Luck is a handy weapon. It excuses errors, and mitigates lack of skill, technique or tactics. It is the last resort of the traditionalist, and the apotheosis of the data-based approach to any sport. But not only is it a handy weapon, it is a deadly one as well.

When a curling free kick hits the woodwork and bounces to safety, that is not bad luck for the striker. It is a very fractional failure in skill. Not that this means that the effort was anything but excellent. Just not quite excellent enough. Something that, the data specialists will explain, can be countered by analytics.

But luck is a powerful adversary. It excuses error, technical and tactical weakness. It is the excuse of the loser, and the humility of the victor. For all that, it is just an extra in the drama of sport.

There is more than luck in holding back the use of analytics in soccer, however. Here are the eight teams who qualified for the

Champions League quarter finals in the 2019/2020 season, and their managers or coaches. (The term seems interchangeable these days).

Manchester City – Pep Guardiola, former professional soccer player, (Guardiola played most of his career Barcelona.)

Lyon – Rudi Garcia, former professional soccer player, (Lille and Caen were among his clubs).

RB Leipzig – Julien Nagelsmann, former professional soccer player, (his promising career was cut short by injury.)

Atletico Madrid – Diego Simeone former professional soccer player, (the tough midfielder had two spells as a player with Atletico during his playing career).

Barcelona – Quique Setien, and prior to that Ernesto Valvere, both former players.

Bayern Munich – Hansi Flick, former professional soccer player, (who also played for Bayern Munich),

Atalanta – Gian Piero Gasperini, former professional soccer player who represented a number of Italian clubs.

Paris St Germain – Thomas Tuchel, former professional soccer player, (another whose career was cut short by injury.)

We could look at almost any set of managers and come to the same conclusion. Soccer is immensely conservative. Managers are drawn from former players. Almost certainly (it is not possible to prove this statistically, owing to an almost non-existent data base from which to work) there are men and women around whose management skills would lend themselves to becoming great soccer managers. But they get no chance. The assumption is that unless the coach of a professional club is an ex player, they will not command the respect of the dressing room. They will not have the know-how to lead training sessions. They will not understand the flow of the game, and therefore be able to make the strategic and tactical decisions which lead to success.

Evidence from other walks of life would question this severely. Not all head teachers come from the ranks of teachers – albeit the same resistance within the teaching profession is often held out towards headteachers without that experience of working in the classroom. Yet, it can work. A headteacher has little direct involvement with teaching, unless it is something they choose to do. Managing an adult is very different to managing a child, or even a classroom of them. Classroom teachers rarely have to make decisions about how to spend a budget or which teacher to appoint. And, just as with soccer managers, a head teacher is surrounded by colleagues on whose expertise they can call.

In business, similarly, a person is appointed for the skills they can bring, not just the experience they have. But soccer is set in its way. And that makes evolution slow. Coaches and managers are appointed very much because of their soccer history; even those who did not play to the highest of professional levels, the likes of Jose Mourinho, Arsene Wenger, or Thomas Tuchel and Julian Nagelsmann from the current younger generation, were professionals themselves. And, of course, during their own careers the use of analytics was unheard. Only now, with younger coaches who ended their careers more recently is there a real openness to the use of analytics. The Premier League in England, for example, has a group of young managers who finished playing relatively recently. Frank Lampard at Chelsea, Mikel Arteta at Arsenal, Ole Gunnar Solskaer at Manchester United, Nuno Espirito Santo at Wolves, Scott Parker at Fulham. To those exciting young managers can be added the likes of Patrick Vieira at Nice, and Steven Gerrard at Glasgow Rangers and a shift in emphasis can be seen when it comes to appointing managers to the dugout. These are former players familiar with the benefits of analytics, which might have both contributed to their appointments in the first place, and certainly means that the growth of the use of analytics is bound to grow. That these young coaches have gained relative success perhaps also reflects their willingness to embrace new technologies.

Soccer is still behind much of the rest of the employment world when it comes to innovation, but it is catching up.

While resistance is still a problem, those opposed to allowing soccer to move on should take a close look at the words of the Bill James. Often referred to as the Godfather when it comes to the use of analytics in sports, he once said the following, which is as applicable to soccer as it is to any other sport, given an open mind by the people in charge.

'In sports, what is true is more powerful than what you believe, because what is true will give you an edge.'

CONCLUSION

Soccer is the most popular sport on the planet. There are many reasons for this. It is a sport that can be the simplest imaginable. All that is needed is a ball, or ball substitute, and a bit of space.

It can be played by almost any person of any age; walking football (soccer) is a growing past time for the elderly wanting to enjoy the competition and physical challenge of a game without risking the sort of injuries that could be serious to an older person. Any child who can walk enjoys kicking a ball.

It is also capable of achieving art form status. At the highest levels, the 'beautiful game' is indeed beautiful. It appeals to the human race's social need, the requirement to belong and share values. It creates heroes and because as the ultimate 'flow sport' it leads to intense debate over almost every aspect. From the relative benefits of 4-4-2 against 4-3-1-2 and so on, to who is the best full back in the league to the tactical errors of the enormously paid coaches charged with running teams.

Analytics are helping to turn gut instinct and opinion into fact. Metrics can now be used to assess almost ever aspect of a players' fitness, well-being, form and technique. Qualitative data is becoming more commonplace, allowing coaches and fans alike to deeply analyse moves and tactics as well as individual performances. Opinions can now be based on evidence, and not just tribal prejudice (not that this will, or should, ever be eradicated altogether); indeed, analytics should never turn the game into a cold, passionless exercise. It is a long way from that as yet. Analytics can increasingly tell us the facts, but not always yet the truth. Maybe that is a good thing. It is the element of the random, the unthinkable, the controversial that makes this wonderful, flawed sport the global joy that it is. Once it becomes just a global business, the game will be diminished. Of course, like so much of our lives, advances in technology drive the use of data in the game.

Analytics have their place, their good side and they are definitely here to stay. But they must always be used enhance the game, not replace it.

For those wanting to read more deeply into the use of analytics in soccer, here are three fine books we can recommend:

Moneyball: The Art of Winning an Unfair Game – Michael Lewis. Ostensibly about basketball, its findings can be transferred – and have been not least in soccer – to almost any sport.

Soccer Analytics: Successful coaching through match analysis – Ian Franks and Mike Hughes. A book ideal for the coach wishing to develop the use of analytics in their own teams, full of useful information and ideas.

The Numbers Game: Why Everything You Know About Soccer Is Wrong – Chris Anderson and David Sally. A very readable look at how data can challenge our preconceptions about soccer.